When you read m  y
spin stories abou ;
you will laugh ar e
challenged and ch 1
immeasurably blessed by the hard-working, straight-talking
East Texan born in a log cabin, and it is both a joy and
a delight to commend his memoir—creatively and aptly
titled God Works in Mischievous Ways. As this pastor-
preacher-administrator (and my former boss!) reflects upon
his life and career in the book's Preface, he muses that 'It
was over all too soon.' I felt the same way regarding his all-
too-brief book about his life—a life transformed by Christ
and the gospel and characterized by visionary leadership and
sacrificial service. It is widely reported that people did what
George W. Truett asked them to do. Unless I miss my bet,
the same thing will be said of Baptist statesman and servant
Paul W. Powell, if it is not being said already!

Todd D. Still, Ph.D.
Charles J. and Eleanor McLerran, DeLancey Dean
and William M. Hinson Professor of Christian Scripture
George W. Truett Theological Seminary

Paul W. Powell rightly deserves the title "Mr. Texas Baptist."
By heritage, character, individuality and leadership no one
else comes close. Born into abject poverty, tried by family
circumstances, early disciplined to hard work, gifted with
an uncanny natural charm and destined for greatness, Paul
Powell's story is better than most current movies. From
limited circumstances he made his way to Baylor with all of
his possessions in a small box and hardly two dimes to rub
together. The teenager who swept the buildings would one

day be chairman of the Baylor University Board and dean of Truett Seminary, named for the only other Baptist who could compete for the title "Mr. Texas Baptist."

Paul moved from a tiny country church to a tiny town church and then a larger town church. At First Baptist San Marcos he found his footing and hammered out the singular style of pastoral leadership that marked him as rarely gifted. This was all the front porch for the big house, Green Acres Baptist Church in Tyler. Paul not only built the largest church in East Texas but one of the largest in the nation. The Green Acres story belongs to Texas Baptist legend. Then Southern Baptists trusted him with their collective retirement at the Annuity Board. Paul demonstrated an unparalleled ability to work with the spectrum of Baptists in challenging times. As if enough worlds had not been conquered, his *alma mater* asked him to be dean of its fledgling seminary. He singlehandedly endowed the seminary and grew its student body from 150-400.

This book is witty, epigrammatic, moving, thrilling and nostalgic. No one who loves Baptist life or preachers will put it down. It is the rarest of things, a Baptist page-turner.

Joel C. Gregory, Ph.D.
Professor of Preaching
George W. Truett Endowed Chair of Preaching and Evangelism
George W. Truett Theological Seminary

GOD *in* WORKS
MISCHIEVOUS
WAYS

a memoir

Paul W. Powell

FLUENCY
TELLING STORIES THAT MATTER

Fluency Organization, Inc.
Design by Diane Kronmeyer and Lindsay Galvin.

Printed in the United States.

Published by Proctor Street Press.

To my family—Cathy, my wife of 62 years,
my children Kent, Mike, Lori and son-in-law Mitchell,
along with my grandchildren Jordan, Katie, and Matt.

.

Table of Contents

Preface

A FEW YEARS AGO I VISITED THE GRAVE OF MY GREAT-GREAT-GRANDFATHER HENRY JACKSON POWELL. He was the first of all my ancestors that I know about to come to Texas. Henry Jackson was born in Mississippi in 1824, but he got to Texas as soon as he could. In 1861 he and his wife, Nancy, and their seven children traveled by oxcart across Mississippi, through Louisiana and on into Texas. It took them six months to make the journey. They intended to settle in Polk County near Livingston, most likely because they had relatives and friends there. But soon after crossing the Sabine River their little girl became ill and they set up camp to tend to her on a nearby piece of land they found with a clear-flowing spring. Henry Jackson bought the property from a man he thought was the owner, only to find out later that he had received a false deed. When the real owner appeared, Henry Jackson had to negotiate buying the land a second time. They eventually had a total of 11 children and raised the entire family there.

A cousin of mine who is into genealogy sent me this information about Henry Jackson, including the fact that he died in 1908 at the age of 84. When I learned that he was buried in the Brookeland Cemetery in Sabine County, something drew me to make a three-hour drive to visit his grave. After walking around on the dry and dusty soil of the cemetery grounds, I eventually found the grave where he and Nancy were buried inside a small, rusty iron fence. Henry Jackson's tombstone was barely legible. I carefully stepped over the short fence to get a closer look and knelt to brush away the layers of mud and sand spattered there by a hundred years of rains. Tears welled up uninvited as I read his epitaph:

"Here I lay my burden down
Changing the cross for a crown."

"Henry Jackson," I said aloud, "I guess you were a believer. If so, you are the only male Powell I know about in my immediate family who had a serious relationship with the Lord. So maybe I'm a preacher today because a long time ago you took up the cross and followed him."

Some time after that day, a friend of ours was telling me about her maid's attempt to quote the familiar line by hymn writer William Cowper: "God moves in mysterious ways, his wonders to perform." The maid had mixed up her words and instead told our friend, "God works in mischievous ways..." The thought came to me that it would make a good title for my memoir, if I ever took time to write it. God works in mischievous or mysterious ways— say it any way you will. God is at work in our lives to bring us to the exact place he wants us to be, and sometimes he does it in the most mischievous ways. Unexpected, surprising, head scratching, confounding, and unexplainable ways.

In the popular television series *Downton Abbey*, Mr. Bates says, "The business of life is the acquisition of memories." I'm not sure I could say that's the whole business of life, but we all acquire a lot of them as we live life, and that's what a memoir is all about. This book is a collection of memories as I recall them. Elie Wiesel, the philosopher, poet, humanitarian, author, and Nobel Laureate who survived the Holocaust, once said, "Without memory, there is no culture. Without memory, there would be no civilization, no society, no future." This is why memoirs are important. They help preserve not only the past but also the future.

I've tried to be honest within these pages. Bob Strauss, former chairman of the Democratic Committee, said, "Every politician wants you to believe he was born in a log cabin that he built himself." Well, I really was born in a log house, but I don't claim to have built it. I just occupied it and enjoyed it. That's the way most of my life has been. I have occupied and enjoyed churches and institutions that someone else built, and I was simply privileged to lead them for a while. I've also tried to avoid self-promotion. George Whitfield, the great evangelist once prayed, "Heavenly Father, for thy dear Son's sake keep me from climbing."

My primary feeling as I look back on my life reminds me of what President Harry Truman said during a visit with British Prime Minister Winston Churchill. They spent some time reminiscing about the past, and Truman wrote in his diary afterward, "It was all over too soon."

Paul W. Powell
September 2016
Tyler, Texas

GOD *in* WORKS
MISCHIEVOUS
WAYS

a memoir

CHAPTER 1

God Can Do Big Things from Small Beginnings

We were poor. But the government never told us we were deprived, and we never thought to ask.

I ADJUSTED MY TIE, TOOK A DEEP BREATH, AND SLOWLY LET IT OUT AS I LOOKED AT THE FACES OF THE AUDIENCE BEFORE ME. I was sitting on the stage of the Ft. Worth Coliseum about to address 10,000 messengers as my second term as the president of the Baptist General Convention of Texas was coming to an end in 1987. It was the height of the Fundamentalist controversy and attendance was at a record high. Every row was packed, every seat taken. Every face I saw would soon be listening to what I had to say.

All I could think about as I stared out at the crowd at the convention center that day was, "Boy…how did *you* ever get here?" Just then, they introduced me and I had to make my way to the podium.

***

Some people will tell you they are from the backwoods, but I really am. I was actually born *in* the backwoods of East Texas in my maternal grandfather's log house—not one of those modern pre-fab kinds but a real pioneer log house in Brookeland, Texas, nestled deep in the Piney Woods. My grandfather had felled the logs, peeled the bark from each one and chinked the cracks between them with a mixture of mud and moss to keep out the wind and rain. As a child, I knew my ancestors had been early pioneer settlers in Texas, but no one ever talked about them. I'm not sure why. Perhaps it was the same reason given by the late Adam Clayton Powell, a black congressman from New York. "I had my family tree looked up," he said, "and then I had it chopped down." Who knows? Maybe there was a horse thief hanging from a limb on our family tree back there somewhere. Considering that large parts of early East Texas were "no man's land" inhabited by outlaws on the run from both the U.S. and Mexico, that could very well be true.

I was born on December 6, 1933, to Jodie and Mary Powell in Brookeland, Texas. To say my birthplace was in the middle of nowhere is an understatement. In anticipation of my birth, they had gone to stay with my mother's parents in Brookeland. When it came time for my delivery, Dad headed for town to get a doctor. However, the red clay roads were muddy and the doctor couldn't make it in time, so my grandfather rolled up his sleeves and delivered me himself. Some of my earliest and fondest memories are our visits to that log home during the first few years of my life. We didn't own a car until I was in junior high, but every summer my mother and my three older sisters traveled by Greyhound bus to Brookeland to spend a week or two with my mom's parents. Dad never went with us.

The first house I can remember our family living in was a dogtrot style on the outskirts of a Texas sawmill town called Wiergate. Our home had an open porch down the middle and two rooms on either side that allowed a cool breeze to blow through on hot summer days. Some of us even slept out there in the summertime to keep cool. Everyone, including my dad, worked for the sawmill. In fact, the Wier Longleaf Lumber Company owned everything in the town named for it—every house, the commissary, the community center, the theater, and the drug store. Just about everything there was. The old B-movies at the theater that changed every week were also provided courtesy of the lumber company. Otherwise my family wouldn't have had the money to go. It was a different day back then. The white folks sat downstairs and the African Americans and Hispanics sat in the balcony, while a foreman alternated floors to keep order. We walked everywhere and had no need for a car. The streets in Wiergate were unpaved, sandy lanes. All the houses were left unpainted, so there was little opportunity to keep up with the Joneses.

When we later moved from the outskirts into town, we upgraded to a home with a cold-water faucet in the kitchen, one drop electric light in each room, and a wood-burning stove where Mom made all our meals. We also had an outdoor privy. Everyone in town used an outhouse in lieu of a sewer system. Every Halloween the favorite prank of the older boys involved going around town overturning the outhouses. It didn't hurt much of anything, unless somebody happened to be sitting in one at the time.

We used coal oil for nearly all our needs—to light the lamps, oil the saws, and even heal small cuts. Whenever I got the croup, mother swore by a cure-all elixir of a spoonful of coal oil and sugar. We were poor, but so was everyone else. We were not one wit ashamed of it, nor did we feel mistreated by society. At Christmas our family received one unwrapped gift left on the porch by Santa Claus. The lumber company also gave every child a small mesh sack with an apple, orange, banana, a few nuts, and some hard candy. There was no emphasis that this holiday celebrated the birth of Jesus. He was never mentioned in our home.

There were six in our family—my mother and dad, my three sisters, and me. Emma and Pat were twins and the oldest. My sister Pat was born deaf and lived at home until she died at age fifty. While Pat couldn't hear, it was Emma who wouldn't listen. She was headstrong from the day she was born. Lillian, whom we affectionately referred to as Punk, short for Pumpkin, was next in line. I was the youngest child.

In our family, Pat always had a special place in everyone's heart. We were uneducated people and had never heard of a school for the deaf. But even if they had known about one, my parents never would have consented for Pat to leave them. Instead, we communicated with Pat using rudimentary hand signals our family developed. Rubbing our thumb and forefinger together meant "money." Waving our fingers across the front of our hairline meant "Daddy" because of his wavy hair. Pulling down on our top teeth meant "Mama" because she had false teeth for as long as I can remember. Resting both hands flat across the heart was "I love you." Because of her handicap, my parents let Pat do whatever she wanted and were always reluctant to discipline her. When she took up smoking as a young child, who could have known that she would one day die from lung cancer?

I never gave thought to what Pat's life was like—a world of silence. As a young boy who found his place playing in the woods every day, it's hard to imagine her never hearing another's voice or the trill of a mockingbird's song. She was naturally the favorite child, but none of us ever resented that fact. I got my tenderness from Mom and my hardness from Dad. But it was Pat who taught me to love and respect people with limitations. Even now, my heart aches as I think of her, and I wish I could hold her and love on her still.

There were no organized sports in a sawmill town. Kids got their own ball teams together and entertained themselves with homemade stilts, slingshot contests, rubber guns, and stick horse races. No one's yard had grass—a blessing since no one had lawnmowers. Any grass in town was chopped with a hoe and occasionally swept with a brush broom. We happily played all our games in the dirt, including a marble game we called "Keeps." We could play marbles six days a week but never on Sunday. The Missionary Baptists in our town held some strange beliefs about it being a game of chance, and I never understood why we couldn't play on Sunday except "they" said so.

Just down the sandy lane from our house was a little Methodist church. My sisters and I attended it once or twice by ourselves as children, more out of curiosity than from any real interest.

For some unknown reason, Dad had no use for preachers or churches, so religion was never part of our childhood. I was actually scared of the church for a long time because he once told me there were ghosts in there. I figured out later Dad was talking about the Holy Ghost. Although I often passed the church on my way to play with my friends, I always sidestepped away from it, keeping my eyes peeled for any "ghost" that might get me.

No doubt God can do great things from small beginnings like mine. He does it all the time. Zechariah 4:10 asks, "For who hath despised the day of small things?" (KJV). Just because you start small doesn't mean that's where you'll end up in life. In reality, there are no small places. There are just places. I learned you can start right where you are today and go most anywhere in the world you want to go. The only limiting factors will be your dreams and your determination.

Of course, you'll have to have courage to seize the opportunities that open up. You'll also need people to help you—and the Lord will bring them into your life, just as he did in mine. But you've got to get up and get to work. To paraphrase Robert Jones Burdette, the world doesn't owe us anything. It got here first. Dreams, determination, courage, and hard work will get you a long way in life, no matter what size place you start from.

There is no substitute for hard work, and it will make up for almost any other deficiency you may have. When I look back on how I learned the value of hard work, I remember my days growing up in a small sawmill town. In every person's life the childhood memories are simple, but they shape our personalities. String them together and you'll have a pretty good idea of what makes a person who they are. As for myself, I was made in the country.

God Works in Mischievous Ways

CHAPTER 2

Hard Work Never Killed Anyone

When I surrendered to preach, no one told me you had to work weekends.

THE OLD LOG HOUSE IN BROOKELAND WHERE I WAS BORN AND WHERE WE VISITED MOM'S RELATIVES DURING THE SUMMER HAD NO ELECTRICITY. Nobody in that county had electricity—no running water, no heat except a fireplace, and no indoor plumbing. It was raw, hardscrabble pioneer living. These are my roots, and they helped me learn the value of a hard day's labor.

While life was difficult for the people living in the backwoods, it was fun for me as a child to visit. I sometimes helped my grandfather and uncles plow with a mule and milk the cows, followed by a long drink of cold water from the well. At the beginning of each day, Grandmother Ada would draw a bucket of water from the well and set it on the porch with a gourd dipper inside so we could all take a drink whenever we wanted. Most of the adults dipped snuff, which meant by mid-morning a light film of black, grainy tobacco threads covered the water's surface. You had to dip deep if you wanted clean water.

Once a week Mother drew a washtub of water and put it in the yard to warm in the sun all day. Then we all bathed that evening using the same communal tub of water. By the time it was the second or third child's turn, you'd have to skim the scum off the top before you got in it. Although I did not spend a lot of time with our extended family, I remember many summers playing with several of my cousins near my age. When the first day of school was out, we took off our shoes and went barefoot and shirtless for the rest of the summer except when we went to town. Even then we still didn't wear shoes.

My parents instilled in me the value of hard work, honesty, self-reliance, and thrift. They taught me discipline and respect for authority—all authority. And they gave me security. It never entered my mind that they wouldn't always be together, although I cannot remember my father ever touching my mother in an affectionate way. I never dreamed that my mother would not be there when I came home from school each day. That certainty gives a kid a sense of well being.

When I turned 14, Dad told me one day, "I want you to go out and get a job."

I swallowed hard and asked, "Where can I get a job?"

He replied, "That's your problem. Just go to work."

So I did. My first job was helping Emma's husband on his ice truck home deliveries for a dollar a day. I planned to work a thousand days and then quit, although I had no idea how long a thousand days could be. Over the years I sold photo settings from house to house, delivered circulars, was a theater usher, and worked for the city sanitation department. I also sold ladies shoes and men's clothes, was a carpenter and a bricklayer's helper, worked as a custodian, and sold and repossessed used cars at Honest Aubrey's Used Cars—"the cleanest used cars in Texas." I was even a waiter in a café for one day.

The local theaters hired boys like me to walk up and down the street, slipping advertisements for upcoming movies in the door handles of the screen doors. It was hot work in the sweltering Texas summers, but I made good money at 25 cents an hour. One day I was especially hot and tired, so I decided to shorten my route by throwing a large bundle of circulars down the storm sewer. A huge rain came soon afterward, and the storm sewer stopped up completely. When city workers cleaned it out, they found it clogged with movie circulars. They informed the theater manager of their discovery, and he called all of us into his office. He said, "If I wanted to, I could find out who did this. But I'll let you go if you'll learn a lesson: 'Be sure your sins will find you out.'" He didn't press it, and I didn't confess it, and I kept my job.

That same manager ended up liking me and even hired me as the head usher with a good raise. I wore a uniform and stood at the top of the darkened aisles with a flashlight to escort people to their seats.

I was not choosy. I took any job I could find. By the time I left high school, we were living in a real house next door to the J.T. Hitt brickyard. The foreman of that brickyard was Mr. Dotey, a Christian man who offered me a job to earn money for college. I soon saved enough money for my first quarter at Baylor University in Waco. Mr. Dotey told me that if I wanted to work when I was home for vacation and holidays I could just show up at the yard. No call was necessary—just be there at 7:00 a.m. and I would always have a job at union wages and time-and-a-half for overtime. I refused to join the union and others threatened me sometimes, but I held my ground and God provided.

***

I've always been a doer, and I think hard work is good for the soul. At my first pastorate in Belfalls, Texas, all they wanted was someone to preach Sunday morning and Sunday evening. I would drive out to Belfalls on Sunday morning, spend the day with one of the members, preach that night and then drive back to Waco each evening. But I took it upon myself to expand my Sunday-only job description to include much more. I thought the church was supposed to reach lost people, so I asked one of the deacons to draw me a map of the homes in the surrounding area. Using a piece of brown wrapping paper, Major Huffines mapped out every road, every lane, and every house for miles in every direction—about 50 homes. Like most people in Belfalls, he knew everyone.

He even offered to tell me which folks attended church and which did not. But I decided I would find out that information for myself. The fact that someone is not interested in God today doesn't mean they won't be tomorrow. Tomorrow they may receive a cancer diagnosis, or someone they love might die in an accident. I've found there are times in everyone's lives when they are more open to the movement of God.

I soon developed a reputation for hard work. That can't hurt you. Throughout my ministry, I visited families who never wound up attending church regularly, but when they had a crisis they called on the only pastor who had ever called on them.

In Belfalls, I also started a church paper, tried to start midweek services (they voted not to do it), planned a cemetery cleaning, and started a recreation program for youth. I even suggested I could move to Belfalls and commute to Waco for school from there. That's how enthusiastic—and foolish—I was. But the church members quickly cautioned me that this was not a good idea. They were a lot smarter than I was. They knew that the average pastorate in that little church was about two years. Besides, all they truly wanted was a Sunday preacher.

One Sunday morning in my youthful enthusiasm I made an unwise proposal to the church. Next door was an old tabernacle—a large, open pavilion with a shingled roof. The years had taken a toll, and there were about as many shingles missing as there were in place. One Sunday in my youthful zeal I said in my sermon, "We ought to either tear that tabernacle down or repair it."

This seemed reasonable to me—tear it down or fix it up. I was giving them two choices. I didn't realize that there was a third option. We could do nothing. When I walked out of the church that day, one of our elderly deacons pulled me aside. "That's the problem with our world today," J.L. Aldridge, a wonderful man, said to me. "You young whippersnappers want to tear down everything we old folks built up." I realized for the first time that people don't always hear what you say or understand what you mean. He didn't want to tear the tabernacle down, and he didn't want to fix it up. He didn't want to do anything. I've since learned that if the preacher will let them, most churches will sit and do nothing and do it very well until Jesus comes. In most of my churches, the people did nothing better than they did anything else.

I thought my ministry was over that day, having crash landed before ever leaving the runway. But I survived Brother Aldridge, and the tabernacle survived me. About six years later while pastoring another church, I received a package in the mail from George Collier, one of the deacons who had overheard that conversation. The package contained a shingle from that old tabernacle. It had finally become so dilapidated that they had to tear it down before it fell down. He wanted me to have a memento of my first encounter with people who didn't want to do anything.

When I surrendered to preach, I didn't know I had to work weekends. But going to church, much less being called to preach, was the farthest thing from my mind when I was young. I could always work hard and do more than my share—and Dad certainly expected me to do so—but neither of us could have known then that I would end up working for the Lord. How that happened is a story in itself.

CHAPTER 3

God Moves When You Least Expect It

Preachers don't come out of the blue;
they come out of the pew.
They come out of people like you.

M Y VISITS TO THE COUNTRY AS A CHILD ALWAYS COINCIDED WITH CANNING SEASON. Mom and her four sisters would can vegetables to consume in the coming winter. They always set aside a few cans to bring to the annual "big meeting"—a 10-day revival at Greenwood Missionary Baptist Church. My mom's relatives went to the revival and brought us along. The revival always included preaching services at night and a Stamps Baxter Singing School in the morning. We rode to every revival meeting in a horse-drawn wagon. With no competition from the radio or television, all the country people came to church whether they were saved or not. The church house filled up, but the men who were not believers stayed outside to visit and pass the time.

Sometimes one or two would walk up to the open windows to look in and listen while the preaching was going on. With one or two exceptions, these would be the only times I went to church until I began attending on my own at the age of 14 back home in Port Arthur. We never went to church as a family—not at Christmas, not at Easter, not for a wedding, not for a funeral, not ever.

The Greenwood Missionary Baptist Church was a little one-room building by a dirt road. The men sat on one side of the church, women on the other, and the young people who were courting sat in the middle section. We sat on homemade wooden slat benches, sang by the light of Coleman lanterns, and fanned ourselves with funeral home fans. When the preacher finished his sermon, if he could talk above a whisper and wasn't walking on three inches of his pants legs, the people felt he hadn't preached a lick.

The final Sunday of the big meeting always closed with dinner on the grounds. The people in the church brought all kinds of food, especially fried chicken and banana pudding, and spread the meal on rough-hewn wood tables erected for that purpose. It was the only time in my life that I got all the banana pudding I wanted. Adults ate first and the children ate last. By the time I was grown, the whole process was reversed so that the children ate first and adults ate last. It seems as if I've been last in line all my life. My only hope is heaven, where "the last shall be first."

When I was 12 years old, I went forward in one of those revival services to tell the preacher I wanted to be a Christian. I was baptized the next Sunday afternoon with some of my cousins in the creek. When summer was over, so was my first blush with religion. I went back home much the same boy I was before.

World War II started on December 7, 1941, when the Japanese bombed Pearl Harbor. About the same time, the lumber company

God Works in Mischievous Ways

had cut all the virgin timber from the area and decided to close the mill. Out of work and out of luck, we moved to another small Texas town called Silsbee to live with my dad's brother until Dad could find a job. Thankfully, older men like my dad were needed to fill the gaps in the shipyards because the young men had gone to war. Uncle Emmet and Dad commuted with several other men from Silsbee to nearby Beaumont to work in the shipyards building oil tankers that were vital to the war effort.

It was difficult and demanding work, and my dad had little time for us when he was home on the weekends. In the afternoons and Saturdays I climbed trees, fished for crawdads in mud holes, and generally played by myself because there was no one else nearby. I kept busy playing with my dog and doing my homework by the faithful coal oil lamp since my uncle's house had no electric lights.

Within a year Dad got another job working for the Gulf Oil refinery in the coastal town of Port Arthur. When we moved there it was the first time in my life to enjoy indoor plumbing, electric lights, and space heaters. The first of the four apartments that we would live in for the next eight years in Port Arthur was a two-story apartment located at 711 ½ Proctor Street on the main street in the heart of downtown.

The five-unit complex was originally an office building above a shoe store. It had been converted into apartments to accommodate the influx of people during the war years. In those days there were no large apartment complexes. The only homes were one-family dwellings, with an occasional duplex or rooming house dotting the neighborhoods. We didn't live in a traditional home until I was in the 11th grade.

It was a three-room apartment—not three bedrooms, just three rooms: one bedroom, a living room, and a kitchen. There were always five of us living in that tiny apartment—Mom, Dad, my two unmarried sisters, and me. Emma had eloped at age 14, and depending on the ever-changing status of her on-again, off-again marriage, she and her two daughters would also move in for a while. Grandmother Dollie on my dad's side rotated living with her children, so there were times when as many as nine of us lived there!

With only one small closet to share, it was fortunate that we didn't have many clothes. I can't remember where we all slept, but I made my bed on the floor under the kitchen table on a small cotton mattress we unrolled each night. Sleeping there was a safety factor: the kitchen was located between the bedroom and the bathroom, and I didn't want to risk getting stepped on by all the comings and goings. When Mom got up early to cook breakfast for Dad, I had to get up and out of the way to make room for Dad to sit down and eat.

Mom was a good housekeeper in Port Arthur, but our apartment was always messy. How could it be otherwise with so many people in it and so little space? As an adult I would develop a fixation on cleanliness. I always kept my cars neat and my churches meticulous—both the building and grounds. I taught our staff and all our people to pick up trash, paper, and cans any time they walked across the parking lot. I believe God's house ought to be the best kept and most attractive property in town.

We had no books in our home—no encyclopedia, no dictionary, no Bible, nothing. If there were any, I never saw them. The Roman philosopher Cicero once said, "A house without books is like a body without a soul." Ours was a soulless house. Dad had only completed the fifth grade and my mother had only completed the third grade, so I suppose we had no need in my family for books. Consequently, I was never a good reader and years later realized I was slightly dyslexic.

One of my most vivid memories is that all the windows of our first apartment faced the brick wall of the building next door. The unit had originally been built with outside windows, but later Grant's department store had been built flush against it. Whenever we looked out our windows, we saw nothing but red bricks. Growing up I could not see anything beyond our drab existence. I had no vision for my life and no purpose beyond the present. I wasn't a reader, and there was no such thing as television. I never had much imagination about the future beyond growing up to be a cowboy or a soldier—things I'd learned from the many movies I'd seen. It was not until later on in high school that the light of hope came into my life. Even then it came slowly. I would have to squint my spiritual eyes in order to realize for the first time that I could become somebody and do something beyond my family's humdrum existence. I could even become a preacher.

When we moved to Port Arthur, I was in the third grade at Franklin Elementary School. The town had an excellent school system, one of the best in the state. As the oil-refining center of the world, money was never an issue with such a large tax base. But Franklin was where all the poor kids like me and Mexicans went. Back then there was no integration or the bussing of students.

A boy born in the backwoods, I grew up running the back alleys of Port Arthur and usually relegated myself to the back of the class in school. Mom was very protective of me and told me one time, "If anybody tries to start a fight with you, you run home." My dad looked up and warned, "If you run home, you'll get a worse whipping when you get here than any boy will give you." I learned to fight early and often in grade school and even got paddled for it once or twice. I eventually grew out of that phase and I was never much trouble at home. The one time I got into trouble with the law was on a Halloween night when a friend and I were walking down the street. He pitched a Coke bottle to me, and it slipped through my hands and broke into a hundred pieces on the ground. About that time a policeman drove by and stopped. After giving us a harsh talking to, he let us go. My dad knew all the policemen from the local bars. When they told him about my Halloween encounter, he came home and told me, "Boy, you get yourself in trouble and you better be able to get yourself out. I'm not going to bail you out."

Life in that seacoast town during the war years was never dull. There were always sailors from some distant port walking the streets, filling the bars, and looking for a good time. Cajuns had migrated over from Louisiana, just like our family, to work in the refineries. I could hear groups of them speaking to each other in a unique version of French on almost any street corner. When the first hurricane hit Port Arthur, the water was so deep because of the poor drainage system that motorboats were running up and down the main street. There were street dances to sell savings bonds for the war effort and always a crowd day and night. When there was a parade, we climbed on the flat roof of our apartment and enjoyed our ringside seats as the bands marched by.

There were no other children my age living in the middle of downtown like I did, so once more I learned to entertain myself. This time, instead of meandering the woods, I wandered in and out of the variety stores nearby and rummaged through their alleyway trash bins. My world was the small few blocks surrounding the apartment and that was all. I set up a cardboard box on a stand and spent hours fast pitching a softball into the box until I could throw strikes with my eyes closed. I made a basketball hoop by bending copper pipe that I found in the trash bins and shot baskets for hours. It never dawned on me that I needed to buy a hoop. First, I had no money and second, I did not know where to get one. After nailing the pipe to a "backboard," I nailed it to one of the posts that ran down the side of our apartment. I cannot recall how I got it up there by myself, but I know for certain that I didn't think of asking my dad for help. I never thought of asking him to help me do anything. There was no animosity between us—he just went his way and I went mine. He had no time for such foolishness as basketball.

I spent time alone, but I never felt alone. There were four movie theaters within three blocks of our house, and I saw every movie that came to town, some of them two and three times. I returned soda bottles to the grocery store for two cents each and shined shoes for 10 cents a pair to earn money for the movies.

Although Grant's department store blocked our view on one side, there was a home laundry on the other side of the unit. The manager of the laundry facility quickly had my number. His uncle was the owner and they were quick to chase me away from loitering on their property or climbing their flat top roof, as I was prone to do. Looking back, the manager might have been nicer to me if he had known I would one day become his son-in-law.

My family always bought the cheapest of everything, including clothes. I wore my clothes (often hand-me-downs) until they were worn out, but it was obvious to me that my classmates were different. I saw what other people had and how they lived, and I was beginning to feel self-conscious about where I lived and how my family lived.

Growing up with parents who went through the Depression, we saved our money and never wasted anything. There were no frills or wasted expenses. I never got over that disposition. Today as a successful retired adult, I wear my clothes until they are well worn. Even today it hurts me to waste money on things I don't think we need. I am deeply imbued with the Depression mentality and have a hard time realizing that I have plenty. My wife and I waste very little and prefer giving to those in need rather than spending on ourselves.

To make matters worse, I was also a poor student and developed feelings of inferiority. To stand before my class or any audience and speak was the most frightening thing I could imagine. My social studies teacher once assigned a research paper that was to be written and then delivered orally. I did my research and wrote my paper, but when it came time to present it to the class I was so nervous that I told her I did not do my work and took a zero rather than stand before the class.

Public speaking makes me nervous even today after 60 years, and I prefer small gatherings. At big events I'm apt to find a quiet corner and stay there, feeling out of place. It's not that I'm unfriendly, and one would never guess that about me as I cover it up very well, but those fears nevertheless are still there and they're rooted in my childhood. I was the most unlikely candidate for the ministry. But then again, God moves in mischievous ways, his wonders to perform. And he was about to perform a big one.

***

The best way to describe my family is that we were civilized pagans. We lived in the shadow of two churches. Just across the alley was the First Christian Church and half a block away was the First Baptist Church—but of course we never attended either of them. My mother was a kind and sweet Christian, but she felt her clothes and lack of education kept her from fitting in at city churches. My dad drank some, cursed a lot, and had absolutely no place for God in his life. He was an honest, hard working, patriotic, conservative—but godless—man. I don't know what happened early in his life, but something caused him to be hostile toward preachers and churches. He often made fun of them, and after I became a preacher he occasionally made fun of me. He never took a drink of whisky (he kept a bottle in the cabinet all the time) without offering me a drink—even after I became a pastor.

I was never into drugs. I never smoked. Never drank. I never committed a crime and was never rebellious. But I was just as lost as any person could be. I was lost in the shadow of the church.

When I was 14 years old, a middle-school friend named Paul Smith began to invite me to church. His parents taught Sunday school at the First Baptist Church, and they arrived early each Sunday to prepare for their class. With time on his hands, Paul would saunter across the street to my apartment and invite me to come back with him. If I was still in bed, my mom would not disturb me. If I was up, she made me go to church with Paul.

I spent some miserable hours trying to stay in bed until I was sure Paul's morning visit had passed so I wouldn't have to go to Sunday school. But Paul kept coming until I eventually went with him one Sunday when he appeared in the doorway of our apartment. My mom had let him in, thinking I was awake. I was out of excuses and agreed to go with him to Sunday school. That's why I don't buy the line, "They know where the church is. They can come if they want to." I knew where every church was. In fact, I lived so close I could have thrown a rock and hit it—and occasionally did—but I never attended services. The church had to come looking for me.

I don't remember much about that first lesson that morning at church, but to my amazement I learned that they had a softball team as well as a basketball team. If you attended three out of four Sundays every month, you could play on those teams. Churches pioneered community youth recreation programs. In

fact, they were at it long before Little League and other nationwide organizations.

I didn't know God and wasn't missing him in my life at the age of 14, but I knew how to play softball and basketball. I was willing to take the religion in order to get the recreation. In time, through the witness and influence of friends, I found something better than religion or recreation: I found redemption in Christ. I experienced God's grace, his amazing grace, and it was the greatest thing that ever happened to me.

At Woodrow Wilson Junior High, the school also had a basketball team and a football team. I longed to play those sports, but I was too timid and insecure to try out for the team. At church, however, they would take anybody—and you didn't even have to try out. Laymen in the church like Elmer Nelson and Joe Prejean were our coaches, and they also took a special interest in me. They didn't know much about basketball and softball, but they loved boys and that was all that was necessary. In many ways, the sports programs in the church and then later in high school were a redeeming factor in my life. Those men meant the world to me. They took me home after practice in high school, talked to me about God, girls, and life and kept up with me until they died.

The whole Bible is a record of God's working in the world. God may move in mysterious or even mischievous ways, but he does move. Jesus said, "My Father is always at his work to this very day, and I, too, am working," John 5:17. And he is still at it.

He is sovereign, so he picks his own place and his own pace. Our ways are not his ways, and our timing is not his timing. Sometimes we must wait until the circumstances are right and our hearts are right. I've learned that he moves through both people and events. When the Lord called young Samuel to be a prophet, Samuel did not recognize God's voice. He thought it was that of his mentor, Eli. It took the wiser and more experienced priest to explain to Samuel who was speaking and how to respond. We are the same way. We often need older, more mature Christians to help us know when God is speaking to us.

Sometimes God moves through dramatic encounters, as with Moses and the burning bush. And sometimes there is just a still, small voice, as it was with the prophet Elijah—and me.

Don't try to hem God in. Give him time and space. Sometimes he moves through Scripture. Sometimes he opens doors. Sometimes he moves through divine impulses. But be assured, God does move. He knows where you are, who you are, and what it will take to make his will known. Then the next move will be up to you. The Bible advises us, "Trust in the LORD with all your heart and lean not on your own understanding; and in all your ways acknowledge him, and he will make your paths straight," Proverbs 3:5–6.

Life would change significantly for me once I entered high school. The biggest wonder God had ever performed in my life up to that point was getting me to darken a church door, albeit it was through a sports program. But he wasn't finished yet. In fact, he was just getting started.

God Works in Mischievous Ways

CHAPTER 4

Obstacles Are Just Opportunities

If you, like Zacchaeus, find yourself up a tree and out on a limb, be assured that Jesus won't saw it off.

FOR SOME REASON I WAS ELECTED PRESIDENT OF THE SOPHOMORE CLASS AT THOMAS JEFFERSON HIGH SCHOOL IN PORT ARTHUR. I had never been well known, but I think the students were tired of the same people being elected to every office and they wanted a change. That's the only explanation I have because up until that time, apart from my activity at church, I was still a wallflower.

The student body also elected Cathy Vaught as class secretary. To me, she was the prettiest girl in the class and way out of my league. Her father was the manager of the home laundry, and I was glad it had been many years since he'd had to shoo me off his property. I was a young man now but still inexperienced when it came to girls.

Our elected roles at school made it necessary for me to get acquainted with Cathy. When I was again chosen to represent the sophomore class as a duke in the annual Senior Ball, I finally mustered up enough courage to ask her to the dance. This would be my first date, and I didn't ask Cathy until two weeks before the ball. I had no idea what all was involved in a girl choosing a dress and getting ready in such a short time. Thankfully she agreed to go with me anyway, and her mother forgave me.

During my sophomore year, my best friend, Weldon Bailey, persuaded me to try out for the basketball team. Unless you were an outstanding player, you started on the "B squad" your first year. I was completely unproven, except for the church basketball league. But somehow I made the starting lineup. The only problem was my aggressiveness. I either fouled out or got thrown out of every game I played. This threatened any hope for me to move up to the varsity team the next year. On the way home from the final game of the season, the head coach of the A squad asked me to sit by him, which was never a good sign.

He started out by saying, "Paul, you're a good basketball player…" and I felt my chest swell. Then he continued, "But you don't have any **** sense. You've got to get control of yourself. You can't score sitting on the bench." I listened and learned. The next year as a junior I not only made the starting lineup but was also elected captain of the team and later named first-team all-district.

A friend, Kenneth McNeese, also asked me to be his assistant as manager of the football team. When he graduated, I became the manager. Sports gave me a newfound sense of self-confidence I'd never had before.

Things were also looking up at home. My family and I

finally moved out of our last of four apartments and into a rental house my junior year in high school. The old home was next to a brickyard where lots of mice lived in the straw placed between the bricks. They often came over to our house and ran in and out of the attic. The first night that Cathy and I stayed there after we were married, she could hardly sleep with those creatures running through our attic. I was used to them and was not bothered at all. Her standard of living had exceeded mine growing up, and I had to chuckle silently when we ate lunch at a church member's home in our first church and she had to use an outdoor privy for the first time in her life. They had a bathroom with a sink and a commode, but our host explained that the water was not hooked up. I was accustomed to this, but it was a whole new world for my dear wife!

All the while I was becoming more active in the church. A number of my friends had committed their lives to serving in the ministry. One day three of us were hitchhiking home from school when Rev. J.O. Morman, pastor of a local church, stopped and offered us a ride. As he drove, one of my friends teased, "We're trying to talk Paul into being a preacher," elbowing me in the ribs and laughing. Rev. Morman, never taking his eyes off the road, simply responded, "You boys leave that alone. That's God's business, not yours." It was not long after that when I did feel the call to preach.

***

I was sitting by myself in the First Baptist Church of Port Arthur one Sunday morning and minding my own business. My life had significantly improved, but I still had no real direction for my future. My only interests were girls and basketball, in that order. It was on an ordinary Sunday, in an ordinary church, listening to an ordinary preacher preach an ordinary sermon, when God did an extraordinary thing in my life. That's the way he ordinarily does it.

Figuratively speaking, Jesus walked down the aisle that day, tapped me on the shoulder, and said, "Paul, come follow me and I'll make you a fisher of men." Like Peter, "I straight way left my nets," albeit mine were basketball nets, and followed him. He didn't have to beg me or bribe me. I did it willingly. And it was one of the greatest decisions of my life. It was a hinge moment, and my whole life swung on it like a door opening to a whole new way of living.

I didn't hear a voice in the night, see a blinding light, or sense any angels in flight. I just had a profound impression about what God wanted me to do. Nothing less than the call of God could have gotten me out of the pew and into the pulpit. People ask me if I'm saying God spoke in an audible voice that day. Oh, no—it was much louder than that. He spoke to my heart. In fact, the impression was so loud and clear that even now, more than 60 years later, if I am still and quiet I can hear it.

I have doubted many things through the years, but I have never doubted that God called me to preach. I believe I was born to preach. It was a part of his plan for my life. Once I made my decision public, several people said to me, "We knew God was going to call you into the ministry." Sometime later, my mother told me that she had always prayed that I would one day be a preacher. I never knew that was the secret desire of her heart until then.

Shortly after I made this decision to enter the ministry, my church elected me as pastor for Youth Week, when the students took over the leadership roles in the church. My first sermon lasted about seven minutes, and that seemed like an eternity. The next time I preached, Brother John M. Wright, my pastor, was

God Works in Mischievous Ways

present in the audience. I confessed to him how nervous I was when I realized he would be listening. He just smiled and said, "Remember, Paul, the Lord is always listening." I never forgot that. And Brother Wright would show up at just the right time, with just the right words, at a critical point many decades later in my ministry.

It's a paradox—my natural shyness and my call to preach. However, I couldn't seem to do anything otherwise. Although I feared public speaking, I found myself looking for opportunities to preach God's Word everywhere I could. I relate to what the reluctant prophet Jeremiah said, "But if I say, 'I will not mention him or speak any more in his name,' his word is in my heart like a fire, a fire shut up in my bones. I am weary of holding it in; indeed, I cannot," Jeremiah 20:9.

I preached every chance I got and never turned down an opportunity. I preached weekly in the local jail, monthly at a nursing home, and as often as possible at a rescue mission in nearby Beaumont. I never turned down an opportunity to preach. My friend Kenneth Williamson and I even went to bars on Houston Avenue in Port Arthur, a seedier side of that seacoast town, and with permission of the bartender we preached to the drunks there. The night my church licensed me to preach, four other boys were licensed with me. Of the five, I would be the only one who stuck with the call and became a minister.

Brother Wright also sent me to preach in various churches that contacted him to fill their pulpits. I preached my first revival meeting at the Mexican mission of the First Baptist Church of Port Arthur in 1952. They paid me five dollars and gave me a copy of the Revised Standard Version of the Bible signed by all 13 members of the church, one of my treasured possessions to this day. The pastor of Calvary Baptist Church in Port Acres, a suburb of Port Arthur, was having voice issues and asked me to preach for him six weeks in a row while he rested his voice. Frankly, the preaching wasn't much and the folks recognized that, but I had a newfound boldness that I can only ascribe to the Holy Spirit inside me.

The threat of failure was there all the while, of course. But the encouragement from others at church or at some of the places I preached went a long way. We just never know how our words are going to affect someone else. I still recall a prominent businessman saying to me after I preached one of my first youth services, "Paul, you're going to make a fine pastor one day." I've never forgotten Fred Ellis for that. Just a word here and there over time is enough to keep a person going. Mr. Ellis and others provided that for me. I didn't understand the change that was happening to me, but God had given me a mission and I set my hand to it.

Spending a large part of my early life alone and hustling for myself had honed an independent streak that served me well. No one pushed me around, but I usually had a smile on my face—something that's probably as true of me now as it ever was back then.

Near my high school graduation, my dad met me on the back porch one day to talk. To my recollection, that was the only extended conversation I ever had with him until I moved out of the house. He looked at me and said, "I'm going to get you a job at the Gulf Refinery."

That was the best job he'd ever had—union wages, retirement benefits, insurance, and good working conditions. He wanted the best for me, but he had a funny way of showing it.

I did not hesitate. I told him, "No, Dad. I'm going to college."

"You don't need to go to college. You've got all the education you need."

"But Dad, you don't understand," I explained. "God has called me to preach." I know now that my dad didn't understand my decision because the Scriptures say, "The natural man receiveth not the things of the Spirit," 1 Corinthians 2:14 (KJV). How could he conceive of God speaking to a person, much less calling someone into the ministry?

With that, my dad said, "Okay, you're on your own. Don't ever ask me for any help."

My dad was not a bad man. He was just tough. That's the way he was raised. That's the way he raised me. Of course, at that time I was just like him. So I said, "Okay. I won't ask," and walked away. I never asked and he never offered.

But God provided. The psalmist says, "When my father and mother forsake me, the Lord will take me up," Psalm 27:10. I can testify that the Lord did for me what he did for the psalmist—he adopted me and took care of all my needs—and quite well. I have always said, "You take care of God's kingdom and God will take care of yours." My parents didn't desert me, but they sent me out on my own and there was no looking back.

***

With no academic encouragement at home, I especially struggled in English. As I left my senior English class one day, my teacher stopped me. Miss Ira Goldman had a reputation as the meanest teacher in school. "Paul," she said, pushing up her glasses on the bridge of her glasses and crossing her arms in a defiant stance. Other students were walking by me, casting their glances my way as she announced, "I know you want to be a preacher and intend to go to college. I just want to tell you, you won't ever make it." I don't know if she was trying to help me face reality or using reverse psychology on me. Regardless of her intent, she motivated me to become a better student. She was right, in part, because I had never really applied myself in high school.

Twenty-five years later I was at Gulf Shores Encampment in Gulfport, Mississippi, when I learned that Miss Goldman, then retired, lived in nearby Brookhaven. I got her address from one of her friends and sent her a package with five books I had written. In my note, I told her I had served nine years as a trustee and had received an honorary doctorate from Mary Hardin Baylor, her alma mater. She wrote back with the nicest note, saying, "Paul, you were always such a good student. I knew you would go far in life." I assumed senility had set in.

It never entered my mind to let either my dad or Miss Goldman deter me. If I'd been in a race, I never would have broken stride. I had a sense of purpose now, and I knew I was smarter than Miss Goldman thought I was. I may not have been book smart, but I was street smart with a good dose of common sense. I never considered not making it. I don't know where I got it from, but deep down I had a foundational confidence in my call, in God, and in myself, no matter what others thought.

I did not fully realize how many odds were stacked against me. Some were staring me in the face, like growing up without God and having to hear Miss. Goldman's prediction about my looming failure. But some obstacles I didn't even learn about until many years later. Turns out, even my four friends I traveled with to seminary every week when I was a student told me long after we had graduated that they had one day gotten together at school and decided I was the one most likely to drop out of the ministry. Forty years after I preached for six weeks in Port Acres as a high school student, I met an elderly man where I was preaching in Louisiana who told me that he'd been a member of the Port Acres church all those years ago. He said he'd told his wife after hearing my first sermon, "That boy will never make it in the ministry." The verdict is still out on that, but it's too late to change it now.

Many of God's servants were hesitant to accept his call. When God called Moses, he excused himself, saying he had a speech impediment. When God called Gideon, he excused himself by saying that he was the smallest member of the poorest family of the most insignificant tribe of Israel. Jeremiah is another. The Lord appeared to him when Jeremiah was a young man and said that he had appointed him as a prophet, but Jeremiah said he was too young for such a position and, besides that, he didn't even know how to speak!

It is easier to fall into a hole than it is to climb out of one. I started in a hole, but I did not have to stay in that hole. I was one of the most unlikely candidates for the ministry there ever was. If I had yielded to my fear and deep insecurities, I would never have been a preacher. Even after 60 years in the pulpit, I still get sweaty palms before I start preaching.

I desperately wanted to prove to my dad and Miss Goldman that I could do it. Hazel Johnson, our youth director at my home church, also kept me busy helping her, including taking a group of us to Ridgecrest Baptist Assembly in North Carolina one summer before graduation. Hazel eventually left the First Baptist Church in Port Arthur and went to the First Baptist Church of Dallas. The last time I saw her she was 90 years old, and we were serving together on a leadership committee for the Baptist General Convention of Texas. It was there that she told me, "Paul, I prayed for you every day."

I know she did. She, along with Brother Wright, were great encouragers in my life. I would need their prayers more than ever before to forge a path to college and my first pastorate.

In life we should expect to encounter obstacles. The Apostle Paul describes wanting to visit his friends in Thessalonica, but

"Satan hindered us," 1 Thessalonians 2:18. The word he uses means to throw up a roadblock in front of a marching army. Satan wants to slow down our momentum whenever we are gaining ground, and he will do anything to hinder us. Circumstances are either stumbling blocks to stop us or stepping stones to motivate us. Psychiatrist and Holocaust survivor Victor Frankl said in *Man's Search for Meaning*, "Everything can be taken from a man but one thing: the last of the human freedoms—to choose one's attitude in any given set of circumstances, to choose one's own way." How we respond to the obstacles we encounter—and everyone will encounter them at some point in life—is up to us. This is how challenges can become assets because they can strengthen us if only we choose the right response to them.

You can't expect God to buy your excuses for not serving him. In the next phase of my life I was about to demonstrate that if I had planned my own life, I would have cheated myself, and so would you.

CHAPTER 5

When God Calls, Answer

Off your seat, on your feet, and into the street.

IN COLLEGE I WOULD HAVE TO BUCKLE DOWN AND GO TO WORK. When I graduated from high school, I had athletic scholarship offers from three colleges. However, my pastor said in no uncertain terms, "You are going to Baylor University." Not only that, Inez Rayford, the wife of Honest Aubrey's Used Cars and a Baylor graduate in the church, told me, "You're going to Baylor if I have to pay your way."

She didn't pay my way, but I did end up attending Baylor. When I left for school, I put all that I owned in a small footlocker. I had three nylon shirts, two pairs of blue jeans, and a suit. I lived on a shoestring—a frayed shoestring at that. After many more mornings at the brickyard, I bought my first car, a 1935 Model A Ford for $35 dollars. All it needed was a water pump, and I drove it maintenance free all summer after my first quarter at school. In the fall, I sold it for $50 dollars. As I look back, I sometimes think I should have been a used car salesman. It pays better and I have the personality for it.

I began reading broadly, although slowly, a discipline I've followed all of my life that helps me to retain much of what I read. The Baptist General Convention provided two-thirds of the tuition for ministerial students at Baylor. The only requirement was to sign a pledge stating that if you ever got out of the ministry you would pay back the money. I signed the pledge with no doubt that I would honor it. (Because of how I was raised, I would have honored it even if I'd ever left the ministry.)

Since I planned to become a preacher, I should have signed up for all the speech courses I could take. However, I was so introverted and grew so nervous thinking about standing up in front of my peers that I only took one speech class. Throughout college I avoided the front row, took notes, and left with hardly anyone noticing I was there. I majored in history after taking a course under Dr. Bob Reid. He had a profound impression on my life then because of his passion for the Lord and for history.

I played freshman basketball my first year at Baylor. A non-scholarship player, I was the fifth or sixth man on the team. At the end of the season Coach Bill Henderson asked me to try out for the team the next year. He said that if I made it, he would give me a scholarship. However, I knew I was never going to be an outstanding player in the college ranks. Besides, by that time Cathy and I had decided to marry, and I was more interested in preaching.

We had been together more or less since the night Cathy and I went to the Senior Ball. That double date with another couple who had a car was the beginning of a wonderful relationship that has lasted more than 62 years with one of God's best women. We

God Works in Mischievous Ways

dated other people off and on through high school, but we always came back to one another. I have made lots of deals in my life involving stocks, bonds, and land, but getting her was the best deal I ever made. As the Scriptures say, "Who can find a virtuous [really good] woman? Her price is far above rubies," Proverbs 31:10. And I had sure found one.

Cathy's mom was never excited about her daughter marrying me. She thought Cathy would be destined to live as a poor preacher's wife and never experience the finer things in life. She would have much preferred that Cathy marry a doctor or a lawyer. However, her dad was altogether different. He liked my desire and determination and was fully supportive of me.

We married on September 2, 1954, at the beginning of my sophomore year in college. After a two-day honeymoon, her parents drove us to Baylor and we unloaded our possessions in a small upstairs apartment. We had no car, and our only income was what I had earned that summer in construction work. We were on our own, but we were not alone.

At Baylor I worked in the maintenance department, sweeping the gym, mopping the bathrooms, and cleaning commodes—all very good training for a preacher. In fact, when I was preaching a revival in Tyler after later serving as president of the Annuity Board of the Southern Baptist Convention (now called GuideStone Financial Resources), a woman who had watched me preach on television told me, "Oh, Brother Powell, I wondered where you were. Someone said that you had gone to that Manurity Board." If only she knew.

I made 75 cents an hour as a janitor, and Cathy made 50 cents an hour working in the school library. That, along with the money I had saved, was more than enough to get us through. No job was beneath me. I didn't need any help, except from God, and he supplied that in abundance. I marked every nickel we spent. The harder I worked, the luckier I became. Call me naïve, but I trusted God and people. We tithed our small earnings all the while, something I had started doing when I became active in church as a teenager. The pastor said we should do it, and I thought I should do what the pastor said. I tithed my first 35 cents an hour salary then, and I'm still at it today.

I was busy with school, work, and my new wife, but I still really wanted to preach. A friend from Baylor I played pickup basketball with pastored a little church in Otto, Texas. When he asked if I would like to preach for him one Sunday when he would be away, I jumped at the chance. Following the morning service, the chairman of his deacons took us home for lunch. Over a meal of homemade fried chicken and mashed potatoes, the chairman told me about his stepson Bill. Bill was the chairman of the deacons at the First Baptist Church of Chilton. They had recently called a pastor, but they needed someone to fill the pulpit each Sunday until he arrived. He asked if I was interested, and I saw a small smile flash across Cathy's face. I couldn't say yes fast enough.

He jotted down Bill's address, shook my hand, and we went home. That night I wrote Bill a letter expressing my interest. Although Chilton was only 25 miles south of Waco, I sent the letter airmail special delivery. Bill soon accepted and invited me to preach.

Bill and his wife took Cathy and me home for lunch on the first day I preached in Chilton. When we took our seats at the table, he shook out his napkin, placed it in his lap, and asked, "Boy, how did you think they were going to deliver that airmail letter to Chilton?" He grinned a wide smile. "Did you think they would fly over, tie it to a rock, and drop it out the window of the plane?"

We all had a good laugh. I hadn't thought of that. I was just anxious to preach. That's when he asked me if I would like to pastor my own church. His friends were members of Belfalls Baptist Church, and they were looking for a pastor. I could hardly sleep that night.

The next week the chairman of the deacons at Belfalls called our home and invited me to preach. Right after I preached my first sermon at Belfalls they called me to be their pastor. I didn't even pray about it and accepted the offer on the spot. I could pray later. They paid me $30 each Sunday. I wasn't worth that much, but I wouldn't work for what I'm worth even today. It was an unusual chain of events that led me to my first church, but from that day until I agreed to serve as the president of the Annuity Board and then finally as the dean of Truett Seminary, I was never without a church. At that time I had been married six months and was a junior at Baylor.

Some people would call the convoluted chain of events that led to my first job as a pastor a coincidence. I call it providence. Remember, God moves in *mischievous* ways, his wonders to perform.

***

After we had been married some time, Cathy's father had mercy on us and gave us a 1946 Chevrolet he'd received in a real estate deal. That made it possible for us to commute 30 miles south of Waco to the church at Belfalls every weekend.

The Belfalls community had a cotton gin, grocery store, beauty shop, blacksmith shop, beer joint, and a Baptist church. That's all any community needs. It was surrounded by some of the best black land farms and farmers in the world. Brother Wright had understood the unique dynamic all country churches share in common and told me to be sure to take a cardboard box in my car every Sunday. He said the farmers would give us corn, peas, and tomatoes in abundance, and we'd need a way to take all of it home. I did and they did, and we ate better than we had since we married.

The little one-room church had a list affixed to the back wall of the sanctuary where members signed up to host the preacher after church on Sundays. We'd go home with different families for lunch and often stay all afternoon. I remember wasting time watching the two comedy hours on television—Oral Roberts' tent revivals and professional wrestling. Then we'd have supper and head back to church for evening worship before returning to Waco that night.

During my first summer at Belfalls we had a 10-day revival meeting. Cathy and I, along with the evangelist, alternated eating lunch and supper at different members' homes each day. We had chicken 20 times in a row, a staple for those good country cooks.

The church left open their double doors during worship for ventilation, as it was not air-conditioned. I was preaching away one morning when Cathy got up and walked out of the service. I saw her out of the corner of my eye just as she walked down the front sidewalk and fainted. I was so caught up in the sermon that I kept right on preaching until some of the men jumped up and went to her aid. She was all right, but she further messed up a sermon that I was sufficiently messing up by myself. Oh, the patience and the grace of good people like those at Belfalls.

That little church only averaged between 40–50 in worship, but they had a significant ministry through the years. It trained many a young preacher who went on to be successful in the work of the Lord. Arthur Rutledge, who served as president of the Home Mission Board of the Southern Baptist Convention, was once their pastor, as was Robert Sloan, former president of Baylor University. Little churches can do a big work, and that one certainly did. Belfalls was a wonderful beginning to a wonderful life of ministry. We loved the church and the people were gracious, as they were in every church where Cathy and I served.

As a result of following Major Huffines' crude map of the area and visiting every home, we baptized nine people in the year and a half I was there. We didn't have a baptistry, so we used the one at the First Baptist Church of Troy six miles away. The first person I ever baptized was a man who weighed more than 400 pounds. Being a rookie, I wanted to make sure we adequately filled the baptistry with water. When I walked out, the water was already up to my waist. When the man got in the water, it was up to my shoulders. I wrapped my arm around him the best I could, and when he went underwater, it was up to my eyeballs. I left the baptistry thinking maybe I needed a scuba diving mask the next time I baptized.

We ended up using the baptistry at Troy more than they were using it. It must have made an impression because when Troy needed a pastor they invited me. In all my years of ministry I never sought a position nor asked anyone to recommend me anywhere. I just did my best where I was and trusted the Lord to use me. Wherever I served, I knew I was there by God's design and his providence.

Paul wrote to his Philippians friends to challenge them to be content in any circumstance (Philippians 4:11). It doesn't matter whether you are serving in a church or sitting in an office—just settle down where you are and trust God who called you in the past to put you where you belong next. When it comes to the pastorate, a lot of guys look for greener pastures when they could water the pasture around them. If you spend your time trying to climb the ecclesiastical ladder of success, you may discover it's leaning against the wrong wall.

I was in a conference years ago at East Texas Baptist University with pastor and Bible scholar Herschel Hobbs. I did the preaching and he did the Bible study. After the service each night we'd go to a café for waffles and we'd talk. He told me about a young man who came to his uncle asking for a recommendation to another church. His uncle said to the boy, "Son, why don't you start a fire where you are. People will see your smoke and come to see what's happening." I had been doing that long before I heard this suggestion. I sent up smoke signals and churches came to me. Becoming the pastor at First Baptist Troy would bring a series of first experiences to this young pastor that proved to be educational, not to mention humbling and humorous.

CHAPTER 6

Leadership Is Learned

*If we would wake up and get up,
the church would fill up, and the world
would sit up and take notice.*

CONDUCTING MY FIRST FUNERAL WAS ONE OF THE MOST
NERVE-RACKING EXPERIENCES I'VE EVER HAD AS A PASTOR.
The deceased was a truck driver who died in a head-on collision.
His truck exploded and he was burned beyond recognition,
leaving behind a wife and two small children. His family held
the service in the sanctuary of the First Baptist Church of
Temple, and it was filled to overflowing. In the midst of this
unspeakably tragic situation, everyone was looking to me to say
something of comfort.

In preparation for the service I had searched everywhere for
help with my message but found nothing of substance. A number
of books contained poetry and selected scriptures, but that wasn't

what I needed. I subconsciously determined that one day I would write a book of funeral sermons to help other preachers. About 15 years later I wrote *Gospel for the Graveside*, followed by four other funeral sermon books—all of which I have given away free to preachers to help them out of the spot I once found myself in. The feedback I've received about these books over the years makes me think they have probably been more help to ministers than anything else I've ever written. Occasionally I have gone to funerals and heard one of my own sermons delivered!

Since that first funeral, I have averaged more than one funeral a month for 62 years. That is 775 funerals to date. I have kept a record of every funeral and wedding where I have presided, a good habit that I recommend young pastors do. My first wedding was in August 1957, and I'm now on #698. When I see couples I've married, I can usually remember them by number, if not by name. I recently married a young couple and was able to talk about presiding at the bride's parents' wedding. The young couple was #696, and her father and mother were #349. When I conduct a wedding ceremony, I usually point to my old pastor's manual containing the names and dates of every wedding I've officiated. I call attention to the fact that the cover is cracked and bent, the edges are frayed, and the pages are held together by tape because it's been through so much. But the important thing is that the book is still together. Someday long after their wedding day, they will get bent of shape with one another and their nerves will be frayed. The only thing that will be holding them together will be the tape of their commitment.

Weddings and funerals are important parts of a pastor's life, and funny things happen all the time. One of the funniest that happened to me was at a wedding when a bridesmaid fainted in the middle of the couple's vows. Not knowing what else to do, the groomsmen picked her up and stretched her out on the front pew. She came to in a few minutes, and they had just helped her back to the platform when she fainted a second time. Once again they stretched her out on the front pew. Again she revived, and they stood her back in place only to see her faint again! They stretched her out on the pew a third time. All the while, I was trying to do a dignified wedding. So this time I said, "Just leave her there. We'll pick her up on our way out." By then I had lost control of the wedding anyway.

I don't know what it is about funerals, but they often take place on cloudy, rainy days. I heard about a funeral for an old lady who had devoted her whole married life to nagging her poor husband. It was raining at the graveside service, and just when the service concluded there was a tremendous lightning bolt accompanied by a burst of thunder. The old man looked at the pastor and calmly said, "Well, she's arrived."

I got to practice more first-time experiences when I went to pastor my second church in Troy, a small town of about 500 people located on I-35 between Waco and Temple. In my first year there I devoted myself wholly to pastoring. I learned to lead a church, conduct funerals, preside at weddings, and improve my preaching. Charles Tope, pastor of First Baptist Belton, took me under his wing and became a wonderful mentor and encourager.

Farmers, local businesspeople, and commuters to Temple comprised the population. Troy also had a good school system that reached for several miles in every direction. Cathy soon took a job teaching high school. I completed my last semester at Baylor by correspondence, graduating in November 1956. The church in Troy averaged about 125 in Sunday school. I later found out that they had intended to pay me less than the $67.50 a week they paid their previous pastor since I was young and still in school. But they changed their mind. We had not discussed my salary before I accepted the call to pastor there, but they assumed I had checked what they paid the last pastor so they felt compelled in the end to pay me the same.

I hadn't checked. In fact, I never became pastor of any church when I knew the salary in advance. After I preached at Green Acres Baptist Church in Tyler, one of the largest Baptist churches in the nation, the chairman of the pastor search committee called me to talk about the salary. I told him I didn't want to talk about it and would take whatever they paid. "I will take care of your spiritual needs, but I expect you take care of my material needs," I added. I don't expect other pastors to function that way, and I don't consider it especially noble, but it's the way I've always operated. And it has served me well.

The Troy church had a small four-room parsonage built on cedar blocks with wall-to-wall linoleum and indoor plumbing. There was no air conditioning, but that didn't bother me, since I had never had an air-conditioned home before anyway. The church was wonderful to us, and we made lifelong friends there as we did in every church we served. I was always fortunate to serve with good people and churches with strong laymen who coached me along.

I continued the outreach practice I began in Belfalls by targeting every street and home in Troy. I asked Jack Dooley Sr., a deacon and the owner of the local grocery store who knew everyone in the area, to visit to with me every Thursday afternoon. Together we drove down every country road and every lane in that surrounding area. We knocked on every door within a few miles of our church. In my five years at Troy we baptized more than 100 people.

Howard Hendricks once said, "You can impress people at a

God Works in Mischievous Ways

distance, but you impact people up close." I found home visitation was the best way to get close to people in a hurry. I recommend that pastors at a new church spend their first year getting to know their people. In a smaller community it's easier to visit everyone and not leave out anyone. After I left Troy, my next pastorate was in a community of 10,000 people. I could no longer visit everyone, but I did cover about one-third of the population in the five years I served there. Making personal visits builds good will in the community, no matter the size. It helps you discover new prospects, brings new people into the kingdom, or plants seeds for a later harvest. It also sets a good example for others.

In those early days I also had to decide if I wanted to preach other men's sermons or develop my own. If I preached other's sermons, I realized that my messages would be much better in the beginning; but 10 years down the road I would not have grown much. I concluded that if I developed my own style, I would become a much more effective preacher in time.

I also made it a point to speak in the language of the people. I didn't know a lot of big words, but I could communicate effectively to the average person. In time I was to learn that preaching is both a gift and a discipline. There are a lot of poor preachers, and some of them don't have any money! On the other hand, good preaching requires hard work. This applies to any talent. If you don't work at it, no matter how gifted you are no one will ever know you had the gift. I was a slow reader with average college grades and a country preacher in small towns, but I was determined to discipline myself to develop my gifts to their full potential.

The Apostle Paul said in 1 Corinthians 1:21, "God was pleased through the foolishness of what was preached to save those who believe." Preaching may seem foolish to some, but it is a tremendously important part of the pastor's work. Preaching is the public part (and in many ways the most satisfying part) of being a pastor. A good sermon well delivered can be exhilarating to the preacher as well as to the congregation. It can produce a spiritual high akin to what an entertainer feels after a performance and may even require time to unwind before being able to sleep.

However, preaching is a small part of being a good pastor. Being a pastor is hard work. For me it meant long days and sleepless nights. If preaching can be exhilarating, pastoring can be exhausting. Paul acknowledged that fact when he noted the perils of missionary service and added, "Besides everything else, I face daily the pressure of my concern for all the churches," 2 Corinthians 11:28. It is the care of the church, if the minister cares at all, that can be draining. As with Paul, these concerns come daily.

I've always believed that after a while the shepherd should smell like the sheep. My goal was always to be a pastor to the people. To me, that means being among the people and being available to them. Remember people's names. Pay attention to children—and stoop down to their level when you talk to them. Tell them they are the most important people at church that day.

In a moderately large church there is always someone dying, someone depressed, someone divorcing, or someone struggling with an addiction to alcohol, drugs, or pornography who needs a pastor's counsel or consolation. In addition there are hospitals, nursing homes, and shut-ins who must be visited, along with weddings and funerals to officiate. I would sometimes come home weary from the weight of the day—dealing with death, visiting sick people in the hospital, and meeting with families going through real struggles in their marriage or with their children.

Then I would go to a deacons' meeting and listen to men bicker over some insignificant, petty decision. It left me discouraged and at times disgusted with how little they understood about the true needs of the church.

When I was the pastor at Green Acres I conducted 40 weddings a year some years, which required me to plan my vacations well in advance. One time when a man called to schedule his daughter's wedding it happened to coincide with my vacation. When I told him I was not available, he became angry and said, "The devil never takes a vacation." I responded, "Yes, and if I never took one I'd be as mean as he is." People often think the pastor should be available whenever they want him, but the pastor and his family have rights and needs too. Besides, as fellow minister Elton Trueblood said, "The man who is always available is not worth much when he is available."

While all of the personal attention to families can wear on a preacher, it can also endear him to his people. They may forget his dynamic sermons, but they will never forget how he helped them in their hard times. Being a minister is wonderful and rewarding work, and after all this time I can say with the Apostle Paul, "I thank Christ Jesus our Lord, who hath enabled me, for that he counted me faithful, putting me into the ministry…" 1 Timothy 1:12 (KJV). He trusted me (believed in me), called me, and enabled me. What a blessing!

***

By the fall of my first year out of college, I was beginning to think I didn't need to go to seminary after all. I told myself I already had a good church that was larger than average size, so why go to seminary for another three years? I knew other preachers who had not gone to seminary and they did okay. However, none had really excelled. That's how ignorant I was and shows just how much I really needed seminary training. Fortunately I had two long-time friends from Port Arthur who were already in seminary and encouraged me to join them. I'll never forget Edmund Lacy and Gerald Williamson telling me, "If you don't go, you will limit yourself. If you do go, you will let God limit you." I went.

The church at Troy was gracious to allow me to go to attend Southwestern Seminary in Forth Worth in the fall of 1957. Several other preachers in the same county joined together in the 135-mile commute. We would drive to Ft. Worth on Tuesday morning for an 8:00 class and then head back home for Wednesday night services. Then it was back to Ft. Worth for an 8:00 class on Thursday and home again on Fridays for the weekend. I did that for three years with lifelong friends who commuted with me: Ed Lacy, Leroy Kemp, Lloyd Elder, Bob Rouse, and Gus Hayworth. I took every course in preaching they offered in seminary, although the professors at Southwestern hardly knew I was there because I once again sat in the back row and neither asked nor answered any questions aloud. Still, I was learning all the while.

For a very brief time in its history, Southwestern Seminary allowed students to earn a degree without taking Hebrew or Greek. I was so poor at languages that I decided to skip them and spend more time concentrating on other subjects. In retrospect I wish I had taken Hebrew or Greek, but I have made extensive use of concordances to study the meaning of words. Shortly after I graduated they eliminated the non-language degree option. I'm convinced the Lord persuaded someone to offer it during that brief period of time just so I could get through seminary. The miracle of parting the Red Sea to let the Children of Israel go through was nothing compared to the miracle of parting the curriculum requirements of Southwestern Seminary so that I could graduate in

1960. God does work in mischievous ways.

After graduation I determined that I would give Troy one full year of service before considering a move. They didn't ask me to do that, but I felt a moral and ethical obligation to do so since they had allowed me to attend seminary on their nickel. On April 28, 1959, our first son, Kent, was born, and a year and a half later on January 31, 1961, our second son, Mike, was born. I wrote my mother a letter every week for 15 years after I left home, but not my father. He asked my mother one time why I never wrote to him. The truth is that I didn't think he would care if I wrote or not. My dad came to see our family once during the 23 years before he died, and my mom came three times in 50 years.

While evangelism and outreach remained a priority with me, we did a lot of other things to improve the church at Troy. I moved my study from the parsonage to the church, established a church library, and built a parking lot, a new educational building, and a new three-bedroom, two-bath brick parsonage. We emphasized recreation and built a lighted volleyball court and started a church softball team. I asked a seamstress in our church to make me a Santa Claus suit and donned it every Christmas Eve to visit every child in our community whether they went to church or not. I took the children candy and promised to be back later that night after they went to bed. I also collected bicycles and other toys, donating them to poor families who lived out in the country. I continued to be a doer, all the while learning how to lead a congregation.

If the pastor can't get excited about what he is doing, he cannot expect the people to do so either. Our enthusiasm comes from our dreams. You can't get excited about nothing. Dreams and goals wake us up and get us up. What worries me most about our churches and ministers today is not our seminary graduates coming out cross-threaded theologically. What worries me most is that so many become discouraged and defeated so early in their ministry. They're just muddling along—no fire, no excitement, no joy, no hope. Paul's admonition to Timothy was to, "stir up the gift of God which is within you," 2 Timothy 1:6. One of our problems is that so many of our preachers have stopped dreaming, and that's why a lot of our churches are nightmares.

I preached a lot of revivals, especially in the summer of 1960. One of the most memorable events brought me to Tyler for a week's revival at a small church called Sylvania Baptist Church. At that time it was a small stucco building on the Henderson Highway. The pastor, Finis Fluker (who could forget a name like that?), strung outdoor lights for an open-air service even though it was mid-August in East Texas and as hot as blazes. I preached my best every night, but only one person—an adult man—came to faith in Christ. I was confident the week was a bust. Little did I know that this trip to Tyler would set a foundation for something 12 years in the future that I could not have imagined then.

CHAPTER 7

Grow Wherever God Plants You

What troubles me about the church today is not that the pews are half full or that the collection plates are half empty but that the people are half hearted.

THEY LIKED ME, BUT THEY THOUGHT I WAS TOO YOUNG TO SERVE AS THEIR PASTOR. That's the message I heard through the religious grapevine (one of the best communication networks in the nation) about the First Baptist Church of Taylor. During the first year after I graduated from seminary, 13 pulpit committees looking for new pastors came to hear me preach and visit with me. However, I had not forgotten my personal commitment to stay in Troy a full year after graduation.

I had been at Troy a year when First Baptist Taylor came to hear me preach. I was immediately interested. The problem was they didn't seem as interested in me. They were accustomed to older pastors, and I was only 26 years old. Nevertheless, they must have gotten past my youthfulness because they eventually asked me to serve as pastor. Kent and Mike were just one and two years old when we moved to Taylor, and Lori was born during our fourth year there.

In 1961 I began five years of happy ministry there in this German-Czechoslovakian city of 10,000 located in the heart of some of the best black land farms in the world. This fertile strip of black land begins in North Texas and stretches all the way to San Antonio and the east side of Interstate 35. Almost everything west of I-35 is limestone and rocks, but the east side is fertile farmland. As Texas was being settled in the early 1800s, a large population of German immigrants who were also good farmers recognized the farmland's potential and decided to settle there.

While Baptists were in the majority in most Texas communities, this was not the case in Taylor. The largest churches were Lutheran, Roman Catholic, and Czech Moravian. The Lutheran church even conducted some services in German, and the Czech Moravian church held services in the local Czech dialect. Even though we averaged only about 250 in Sunday school, the church's influence was out of proportion to its size. We were small, but we were the largest Baptist church in Williamson County! Up until that time I had not been involved in the Texas Baptist Convention due to my school commitments and the fact that Cathy and I did not have extra money to travel to the meetings. In those days I would have made a good independent Baptist because I was content to work my own patch. But I began attending convention meetings with some of the laypeople at our church who were already very involved with Texas Baptists. I got my first glimpse of a worldwide ministry and my responsibility to help reach the world for Christ. One of the debts I owe to Texas Baptists is not only giving me a world vision but also a means of achieving that vision.

Cecil Sherman, who worked in the evangelism division of our state convention, once conducted an associational conference in our church. I will never forget him asking the group of pastors assembled there, "What did you think God called you to do when you surrendered for the ministry?"

No one responded.

Since I was the host pastor, Cecil turned to me and asked, "Paul, what did you think he was calling *you* to do?"

"I thought he was calling me to preach the gospel and win the lost," I told him.

Cecil smiled and asked, "Why don't you spend the rest of your life doing that?"

I decided in that moment that this was exactly what I would do, and I have never wavered from my decision.

I continued my emphasis on outreach and house-to-house visitation in Taylor, but of course I could not visit everyone in a community of 10,000 people. I set aside every Thursday afternoon to visit as many homes as possible, not skipping any doors.

I walked up to a shack of a house in Taylor one day and quickly concluded that surely no one lived there. But I had promised myself to knock on every door, so I did. After a moment a shabbily dressed woman came to the door.

"Hello, ma'am," I said and introduced myself. "I'm out visiting to get to know people. Do you go to church anywhere?"

Embarrassed, she looked down at the floor and replied, "I would go to church, but I don't have any nice clothes to wear. And I don't have a way of getting there anyway." I quietly recalled my own mother saying that she would feel out of place at a nice church and felt compelled to help this woman. God doesn't want any homeless children. Every Christian needs a church home.

After we visited a while, I asked her if it would be okay if one of the ladies in our church helped her. She agreed and I asked one of our ladies who lived a few blocks down the street from her to assist this woman.

The next Sunday the woman was in church. The next Sunday she was in church again. As she left that second Sunday, I asked if I could come by Thursday and talk with her again. She smiled brightly and said, "Yes sir, that sounds just fine."

That Thursday we sat by the light of a kerosene lamp inside her run-down home as I read the Scriptures to her regarding sin and salvation. We prayed together and she invited Christ into her life. Without me even suggesting it, she said, "Pastor, I'll be in church Sunday and I want you to baptize me." On Saturday night she died, and Monday morning I buried her. But I buried her as a believer. I firmly believe that if a pastor is going to be effective in a church, he needs to ring doorbells as well as church bells. It can make all the difference in one person's life.

***

I determined long ago that if no one else in the church did what he or she ought to do, I would. I also realized early on that there was a greater probability of others going to work for Christ if they first knew I was working. I'm not sure if I had realistic expectations about churches in those early days, but I became very discouraged at Taylor because we weren't reaching as many people for Christ as I thought we should be reaching. The church wasn't growing like I thought it should grow, and I also felt that the deacons were not doing their part. I shared my concerns with our deacons in a meeting one night. After I finished talking, the room

God Works in Mischievous Ways

was silent. Then Deacon Joe Green spoke up and said, "Pastor, some of us aren't sure that you really love us."

I was stunned. I determined that night that they would never have to wonder again if I loved them. I've heard that you don't get a second chance to make a good first impression, but Joe was a good man and gave me that opportunity. One thing I began doing as a result of what Joe said was writing notes to people, a practice I've kept my entire life. Note writing can be a powerful force in ministering to others. I recommend it to all those in ministry because there is no substitute for sending a quick note to people you appreciate—and no excuse not to do so. Consider the story of George W. Truett, who at the invitation of Woodrow Wilson spent six months in Europe during WWI ministering to the troops. He often worked 18-hour days, preaching as many as six times a day to 15,000 men. Still, he found time in the evenings to write a personal note to the families of every Texas boy he met. As you can imagine, that act endeared him to those families forever, and they told everyone they knew what he had done.

I always kept a good supply of thank-you notes handy. I wrote notes for dinner engagements and for volunteering at the church. Whenever people did me a favor, big or small, I was quick to express my appreciation. At times people would bring us a pie or homemade candy and say, "Now preacher, you don't have to write me a thank you note for this."

But I would reply, "Yes, I do. I am determined gratitude will not die in me, and the only way to keep it alive is to express it." I've heard that when the English novelist Rudyard Kipling was at the height of his popularity, it was said he received 25 cents for every word he wrote. Some speculative person wrote him a letter with a quarter enclosed with the request, "Send me one of your best words." Kipling responded with a one-word note, "Thanks."

That will be one of your best words too.

I also wrote people on special occasions, such as a 50th wedding anniversary or a milestone birthday. At the start of the holiday season I also wrote those who had lost a loved one that year to let them know I remembered them. The holidays are the hardest time of the year when you've lost someone you love. A simple note not only comforted people but also endeared me to them forever. I set aside the week before Christmas to visit every shut-in in the church. My shut-ins loved it. I did not do it to impress anyone—it was just the right thing to do. Like the families who received notes from Truett, these dear shut-ins told everyone about "the preacher's visit." When you go out of your way in Jesus' name, word gets around and people soon know who and what you are. By the time I left Taylor I felt I'd made sure that all the members in the church knew I loved them. In return most of them loved me and my family back and still do to this day, more than 50 years later.

I don't lie, but I have been known to stretch the truth on occasions. One time a lady in the church brought me a pecan pie. I love pecan pie, but this was the worst pie I had ever attempted to eat. It was so hard it would have made a better steppingstone in the back yard. Then I made the mistake of telling her how good it was in my thank you note to her. In a few weeks she brought me another one. I'm telling the truth when I say she had not reached the corner in her car when I took the pie to the garbage can and threw it away. The next Sunday she asked how I liked the pie. I responded, "Your pies sure don't last long around our house." I know I was being deceptive, but let the man who is without sin cast the first steppingstone.

In Taylor, as in all my churches, I continued to be a doer. Some of my ideas I picked up from talking to other pastors, and some I thought of on my own. I was always on the alert for new ways to reach people for Christ and do a better job. The church started a softball team and entered the city league. The young couples got together for volleyball and played each other on Friday nights. We also started weekly services in the local nursing home and in the city jail on Sunday afternoons. No stranger to jail ministry, I took a group of church members with me including J.E. Moore, who picked the guitar and sang two or three old songs to our captive audience. Then I would share the gospel.

One Sunday at the jail I turned to Ross Baldwin, the high school principal, and said, "Ross, you share with the men today." I am not sure if I caught him off guard, but he shared with the men exactly what I had been sharing for the past several months. He had listened, absorbed it subconsciously, and repeated back what I said.

Ross commented later, "Pastor, before we started going to the jail I couldn't share my faith at all. Now I can share it with anybody, anywhere, anytime." I could not help but wonder what would have happened if no one had ever asked Ross to share his faith. Most Christians want to sit, soak, and sour until the Second Coming. You can sit in a pew until you mildew. We need to be serving. It's amazing what people will do when you ask them. Pastors must challenge people to share their faith. Some people never share the gospel with others because no one has ever personally challenged them to do it. Some people are waiting to be challenged, and when they are they will rise to the occasion.

I also made efforts to connect with the larger community outside of church. No other preacher was doing that, but how can you reach a community if you don't mix and mingle with it? I joined the Rotary Club. I also asked the editor of the local newspaper if I could write a religious column each week. My column was entitled "Everyday Christianity," and it marked the beginning of writing a weekly column for newspapers not only in Taylor but also in San Marcos and Tyler for the next 25 years. We began broadcasting our Sunday morning services over a local radio station that reached that whole area. Things were going well, but I would soon learn that not everything I did met with widespread approval.

CHAPTER 8

Conflict Is Inevitable

*There are two kinds of pain: you can
have one or you can be one.
Some Christians are so mean that
if they were in the arena with the lions,
I'd pull for the lions.*

I OCCASIONALLY RODE ON FRIDAY NIGHTS WITH MY FRIEND AND LOCAL HIGHWAY PATROLMAN NORMAN AUTRY AS HE CHASED DOWN SPEEDERS AND DRUNKS. We'd sometimes stop at a local bar about 2:00 a.m. for a cup of coffee. This incurred criticism, especially from some of the older ladies in the church who thought their preacher shouldn't be seen in a place like that. I don't know why they worried; no respectable person was there anyway.

I always felt that a preacher needs to keep his feet in the mud as well as his head in the clouds. I didn't want to be so heavenly minded that I was of no earthly good. Besides, when God called me to preach, he didn't drain the red blood out of my veins and fill them with buttermilk.

A very highly educated alcoholic began listening to our services on the radio, and we became friends when he started attending our church. Through that friendship I began working with a group of alcoholics, eating breakfast together at a local café once a week. This also upset some people who thought this was beneath the dignity of their pastor. But I reminded them that Jesus stayed in holy hot water for associating with sinners and was even called their friend. He said, "It is not the healthy who need a doctor, but the sick," Mark 2:17. This group of men was sin sick, and they needed Christ and the church. So I stayed at it and enjoyed seeing them all sitting together on the back row on Sunday nights at church. I even jokingly called their pew "skid row."

We also planned an annual watch party on New Year's Eve. As part of the activities the first year we wanted to have a domino tournament. But some of the older people said that we shouldn't play dominos in the church. The parsonage was adjacent to the church, so I just moved the domino tournament into our house until it was time for worship back at the church! That seemed to satisfy those who had complained, especially those who joined in the games at our home.

The Taylor mayor's son was a wild kid. Whenever the police gave him a ticket, he would tear it up and throw the pieces in their faces. The chief of police worked for the mayor, leaving him little recourse. Word of this injustice came to me, and I said in one of our radio broadcasts that the police ought to enforce the law "even if it was the mayor's son."

I was at the local bank a couple of days later when the president of the bank pulled me aside. "Paul," he warned, "the mayor said he was going to run you out of town." One of the good things about pastoring in a small town is that it's not far to the city limits.

I have followed a lifelong pattern of not avoiding confrontation. Whenever someone had a disagreement with me, I preferred to meet face to face, settle the matter, and move forward. The Bible says, "If it is possible, as far as it depends on you, live at peace with everyone," Romans 12:18. Since the mayor's office was just across the street from the bank, I walked over to see him. I greeted the mayor and said, "Mr. Mayor, I understand you wanted to see me."

He closed the door to his office and responded with some choice words about what I had to say in my sermon.

"Mr. Mayor, if it's not true, I'll apologize. If it is true, I'll stand by it," I said.

What could he say? To make a long story short, the mayor didn't hold it against me, and we continued to be friends.

I shrugged off these minor criticisms, but they were nothing compared to my first few lessons in denominational politics. The first lesson came years later, when the president of Mary Hardin Baylor retired and I was asked to serve on the presidential search committee. At that time Mary Hardin Baylor was an all-girls school, and most of the alumni intended for it to stay that way. Leonard Holloway, the new president we elected, raised some eyebrows when he started a movement to make the school co-ed. I was asked to serve on the committee to study this proposal, and we recommended that Mary Hardin Baylor become co-ed. That decision infuriated some of the older graduates, and they let their displeasure be known. But this decision to become co-ed ultimately saved the school. Somehow I survived the wrath of some of those dear ladies, and in time Mary Hardin Baylor even gave me an honorary doctorate.

Another time when I was the chairman of the administrative committee for a large Baptist ministry in Texas, I was disheartened to hear charges of dishonest behavior regarding the administrator. When I went to him in private and asked him to explain his actions, he could not (or at least would not) do so. When our committee investigated the charges and found them to be true, I notified the board of our findings and our intent to call a special meeting to hear our recommendation to terminate him. However, he had a number of close friends on the board who were busy building support for him while we were collecting evidence against him. When the board met to consider our recommendation, one of his friends stood and said, "I recommend that we not hear the report of the administrative committee and that the meeting be adjourned." Before I could blink, the chairman called for the vote, the motion passed, and the meeting was adjourned. The lesson was, as it is in all of politics, "Forget the facts and get the votes."

But that wasn't the end of the story. A few weeks later one of the most influential supporters of the administrator asked me to lunch. He said, "Paul, you're a good preacher with a bright future, but if you don't change your ways I will see to it that you will never go anywhere in this denomination."

I expressed my appreciation for his concern about my career, but I told him I would just keep doing what I thought was right and entrust my future to God. I developed a reputation from that incident among some people, and it was not a good one. The rumor was that I was a troublemaker, and this false assumption followed me among some people for many years.

More than 30 years later, when I was serving as president of the Annuity Board, I ran into another influential man from that camp while attending a meeting in Nashville. Referencing my position in Baptist life at that point, he said to me, "I'm glad you've changed your ways."

I shook my head and said, "Friend, I hate to disappoint you. But I haven't changed my ways all that much. What I did was right." In fact, the man we had recommended for termination was forced to resign two years later—not only from that position but also from his next job as well. I think time vindicated my committee's recommendations, but I'm not sure it has vindicated my reputation!

I prefer peace and harmony, but I am plain spoken. Often too outspoken. If you talk to me long enough, I'll tell you exactly how I feel. Some people thrive on adrenaline and seek danger scaling mountains and jumping out of airplanes as a way of feeling important and alive. Others seek confrontation for much the same reasons. I've found that fundamentalists are that way, dogmatically holding to their own opinions and constantly needing an enemy to fight. Some people cannot function without conflict.

Not me. I have never sought confrontation—but I have not shied away from it either. I always dealt with confrontation out of principle over any other reason. The Bible says the "righteous are as bold as a lion," Proverbs 28:1. I don't know where my boldness came from, unless it was the Lord. (I don't blame as much on God as I used to.) I agree with what Paul said to Timothy about being bold, "For God did not give us a spirit of timidity, but a spirit of power, of love, and of self-discipline," 2 Timothy 1:7.

After five years in Taylor, God began preparing me to make another move. Several pulpit committees had heard me preach at Taylor, but they weren't all interested in me. And I wasn't interested in any of them until First Baptist San Marcos came along. From the time I heard about their pending visit, I felt that was the place I ought to go.

At that time San Marcos was a college community of about 20,000 people located between Austin and San Antonio. It was the home of Southwest Texas State University (now Texas State University), the alma mater of President Lyndon B. Johnson, and had an enrollment of about 7,500 students. In addition there were 3,000 students at Camp Gary Job Corps Training Center, a vocational training program that was part of our government's war on poverty. It was also the home of a Baptist prep school called San Marcos Baptist Academy. During the school year San Marcos was bustling with activity, but during the summer and on holidays it was peaceful and quiet.

The pastor search committee invited me for a visit but made no contact with me afterward. I later learned that one member of the committee wanted his cousin who had played football at Southwest Texas State to be their pastor. His influence eventually prevailed in the committee, and they invited his cousin to preach "in view of a call" when the church would vote on whether or not to accept him as their pastor. This democratic process is how Baptist churches get their pastors. As it turns out, they voted for him to become their pastor, but he did not get the percentage of votes he wanted. So he declined the invitation.

The search committee was now back to square one. I continued to have strong feelings about the church in San Marcos, but I had long since asked that my name be removed from consideration. Months passed. One Sunday two new pulpit committees sat in our services at Taylor. One was from First Baptist Athens, and the other was from First Baptist Gatesville. I left town after church that day to preach an evening revival meeting in Temple. The next morning I received a call from both committees asking me to meet with them and consider becoming their pastor.

Later that morning I received a third call. It was the chairman of the search committee in San Marcos asking to meet with me for lunch. He was a salesman and explained that he had just been talking with a customer that morning about their need for a good pastor.

"You don't have anyone you'd recommend, do you?" he'd asked his customer. The customer recommended me!

It just so happened that I'd been to the First Baptist Church in Belton (his customer's church) just the week before to speak at a banquet. Before we finished lunch the chairman had invited me to preach in San Marcos in view of a call—one more instance of God moving in his mischievous ways.

God Works in Mischievous Ways

CHAPTER 9

Stay the Course

It is in the trenches that the ministry pinches.

T<small>WO DAYS AFTER I ACCEPTED THE CALL FROM SAN MARCOS TO BE</small> <small>THEIR PASTOR, I RECEIVED A PHONE CALL FROM THE DIRECTOR</small> OF THE OFFICE OF ECONOMIC OPPORTUNITY, A PART OF OUR FEDERAL GOVERNMENT'S WAR ON POVERTY. He wanted to meet me at the Driscoll Hotel in Austin for lunch. I arrived early and stood outside the hotel awaiting his arrival. Soon a big black limousine pulled up. A chauffeur in a black uniform and cap hopped out and opened the back door for the director. I thought to myself, "If this is the way we fight the war on poverty, I think I'll join up."

Leadership from the world's perspective is markedly different from leadership in the church. The pastor is to be a servant—a servant leader. Remember, Jesus said he came to serve, not to be served. There is always the temptation for a leader to start as a servant and wind up acting like a celebrity.

When the pastor does not lead, the church does not act. A good leader sees what needs to be done, figures out how to do it, makes a proposal for the church to act on, and inspires the people to follow him. Some people make leadership very complicated, when it really only requires four things. First, leaders need a vision to see what needs to be done. Second, they need wisdom to know how it can be done. Third, they need the courage to act by proposing that it be done so the people can act. Fourth, they must have the trust of the people to follow him in getting it done. Vision, wisdom, courage, and trust. These are the four qualities of good leadership.

In San Marcos I continued to be an unapologetic advocate of church growth. Everything that is alive grows. If it doesn't grow, it dies. Churches need to be growing numerically when possible and ever and always growing spiritually. I emphasized outreach so much that at the end of six years we were baptizing 100 people a year.

The church in San Marcos had been completed in 1930, but due to the Great Depression the church had defaulted on its bond payments. This longstanding financial failure had cast a pall over the church, and it was hesitant to venture out. The previous pastor had wisely led them to provide some much-needed space, but more was still needed. While San Marcos was expanding in every area, especially the university, the church was talking about building an additional building to meet their needs. But that's all it was at that point—talk. I met with the long-range planning committee, and after some discussion, I got to the heart of the matter. I told them, "If our church is going to grow, we *must* build this building."

The chairman of the committee casually responded, "Who said we wanted to grow?"

What a question! I said to him and to the committee, "If you ever officially decide that, let me know and I'll be out of here. I have only one life to live, and I don't intend to waste it on people who don't want to do anything."

It wasn't the first time I had encountered resistance, harkening back to my days in Belfalls when I'd challenged them to address the old tabernacle. But it was the first time I realized that not every church *wanted* to grow. I've since learned that the goal of most churches is to meet next Sunday, and they are always reaching their goal.

I later discovered through the grapevine that the chairman's remarks had a context. Apparently he had something against me. As I've said, I never let grievances fester. I've also learned never to accuse a person when dealing with conflict. I simply open the conversation by asking, "Is there some contention between us?" That usually gets the conversation going in the right direction, even if it is a difficult course. They have to tell you the truth, or they will have to lie.

If a person denies having an issue with you, but you've heard otherwise, I've found it helpful to follow up by saying, "This is what I've heard, and I thought we ought to talk about it." Then explain your understanding of the situation.

As was my custom, I thought I should visit the chairman privately. He had a retirement benefit, a full-time job, and two small side businesses. I caught him at one of them on a Sunday afternoon working in his shop.

"Is there some contention between us?" I asked after a brief greeting.

"No," he responded, folding his hands across his middle. "You're the kind of pastor we need, but you're not the kind I like."

Once again, I was intrigued by his candor. I said, "What kind do you like?"

"I just want to get up, go to church, go home, and not be bothered."

He was honest—I had to give him that. But I also had to tell him the bad news. "As long as I'm here," I assured him, "you're going to be bothered."

The truth is, he didn't dislike me. He disliked being disturbed. He had not yet realized it was the responsibility of a pastor to comfort the disturbed and disturb the comfortable. And that inevitably leads to conflict.

Keep in mind that I pastored in San Marcos during the turbulent years of the Vietnam War. We were a nation of conflict. The university in San Marcos was not immune to the riots and student protests occurring on campuses throughout America at that time. More than one parent contacted me concerning a child who had come to college, gotten into drugs, and dropped out of school. In response to one mother's particularly poignant plea for help, I searched out a young man and found him living in a mobile home. The front yard was a veritable junkyard with a 50-gallon oil barrel, old automobile tires, cans, bottles, and trash strewn about. I picked my way through the minefield of debris and knocked on the metal door of the mobile home. A stringy-haired kid in ragged clothes finally answered.

After a brief conversation about who I was and what I was doing there, I got to the point and asked him, "Son, what do you want to do with your life?"

He straightened and responded with a sense of nobility, "I want to go to Florida and clean up the Everglades."

I'd always practiced a quick wit, something I inherited from my dad, so I retorted, "If you want to clean up something, why don't you start in your own front yard?" He didn't have much to say after that.

Leaders challenge people to take a look around and change the status quo—even if doing so makes them uncomfortable. And even if it leads to conflict.

I remember a deacons' meeting in San Marcos where we

were discussing giving financial aid to a mission church in Reno, Nevada. We talked for 40 agonizing minutes and finally arrived at the idea of giving them $50 a month. Then someone said, "We need to act on faith." One of our deacons who seldom came to a meeting spoke up and said rather piously, "Well, if you're going to act by faith, I make a motion that we double the amount." By then everyone was worn down by the discussion, so somebody mercifully seconded the motion and it passed.

The man who made the motion was a million-dollar-a-year insurance salesman, and his picture often appeared in the newspaper saying so. I also knew that he gave almost nothing to the church. For the first time in my ministry I had looked up his giving record after he made the motion to "act in faith" that evening. His gifts amounted to just a few dollars. I called on him at his office the next day and said, "I want to commend you on your motion last night to increase our gifts to missions. I have looked up your giving record, and I think you ought to give all that extra money yourself." It would just about triple his gifts to the church that year, but he agreed to do it.

On another occasion we were discussing the need for a new building. One of the college professors whom many people knew gave almost nothing to the church was quite vocal in his opposition. As a result of his resistance, the proposal was voted down. I took him to lunch the next day and told him that I did not appreciate him trying to tell the church how to spend money he did not give. He was quiet in business meetings after that!

One of the worst things that can be said of a preacher is that he came and went and no one noticed. In fact, one of my maxims has long been, "I'd rather be 'cussed' than not discussed at all." That was true of me in every place I served but never more so than in San Marcos.

However, not everything was conflict and confrontation. In fact, my time there was very rewarding on many levels. I took my first overseas trip with San Marcos to Uganda in East Africa to participate in a revival. On another occasion the church sent me to Reno, Nevada, to visit the mission church we helped support. One of the deacons in the Reno church wanted to take me to a casino to play the slot machines. I told him I had never gambled, and I didn't intend to start on that trip. But then he mentioned Louis Armstrong would be playing, and he had tickets, so I confess I yielded to temptation.

The deacon immediately purchased a roll of nickels at the casino, handed them to me, and said, "Here. Now you've got nothing invested and nothing to lose. You can't leave here without just trying the slot machines." I put a few nickels in the machine and lo and behold I hit the jackpot! I put the money in my pocket and left a winner, but the sad thing is that I couldn't tell anybody about it back home. This is my first public disclosure about my last taste of gambling.

I also enjoyed making some lifelong relationships in San Marcos. Every town usually has its own standout character, and Milton Jowers was that person in San Marcos. He had coached the high school team to a state championship before there were class divisions. He then became the head coach of Southwest Texas State University for both football and basketball, winning numerous conference championships and taking the basketball team to the national finals. Coach Jowers was a hard-nosed ex-Marine who intimidated everybody—and I mean everybody—including his players, the administration, and the community.

By the time I got to know Coach Jowers he was the athletic director. A few months earlier I had led his head basketball coach, Vernon McDonald, to faith in Christ. Vernon then became

God Works in Mischievous Ways

concerned about the spiritual state of all his fellow coaches. He was on me continually about witnessing to this one and that one. He finally got around to challenging me one day to visit Coach Jowers. When I hesitated for a split second, he leaned back in his chair and smiled. "You are a double dog coward," he taunted, which was like saying "sic 'em" to a dog. Of course I would visit him, I told him. Vernon joked, "I expect you'll do okay if you have guts enough to try. And Coach Jowers doesn't bite your head off."

I've always related to men throughout my ministry. I hid many of my lifelong fears and insecurities in order to present an image of courage and competence. Among his disciples Christ set the example of what it means to be a man. God used my natural affinity for sports in high school and college to help me establish a common bond with men. The fact that I did not grow up in a religious home actually worked in my favor to connect with other men like my father who had no use for God. I was always direct but not abrasive in conversations with other men when it came to their salvation.

I went to see Coach Jowers at his office the next day. I knocked on his door and entered after he issued a terse, "Come in!" I introduced myself and told him I had come to talk with him about his soul. The last thing I saw as I closed the door to Coach Jowers' office were Vernon's eyes wide in disbelief.

We visited a great while, and as I left Coach Jowers told me, "If you care enough about me to come see me, I'll be in church Sunday." And he was. Several weeks later he and his wife professed faith in Christ and wanted to get baptized. I'll never forget taking his hand that day and Coach Jowers saying, "Preacher, don't put me on the bench. I want in the game." He wanted to be a player, not a spectator in the church. True to his word, he got in the game and stayed in the game until his death. When he died I returned to San Marcos to conduct his funeral.

It's easy to get discouraged in the ministry because we often don't know for many years the good we've done, and sometimes we never know. That, by the way, is why God's judgment will not come until the end of time and the complete record is known.

***

One of the worst and at the same time best experiences of my life happened to me in the early 1970s at San Marcos. Like Christian in *Pilgrim's Progress*, I fell headlong into the "pit of despair." I'm not talking about discouragement. I mean a deep depression. I felt completely overwhelmed by a sense of hopelessness and fear. For someone who had been optimistic all of his life up to that point, I didn't understand what was happening to me or why.

Looking back, I've tried to analyze what brought me to that frightening place, and I've decided that several factors contributed to my depression. One, I was working too hard. I'm not sure if I was working out of a deep dedication to God or subconsciously trying to prove something to myself, my dad, or even to Miss Goldman. Whatever the reason, I was keeping very long hours, staying up late working and getting up early to do it all over again.

I also harbored a deep anger and frustration at one of my staff members who was divisive and disloyal. I should have fired him, but that is easier said than done. It got to a point where my anger made me physically sick and I developed an ulcer. Ironically, this staff member also had an ulcer, and I didn't want anything he had. I let the ulcer eat at me in more ways than one because it also shattered my ego. I thought I was the kind of person who gave ulcers, not the kind who got them. I became convinced that I'd have this pain the rest of my life, not knowing that you could get over an ulcer in a couple of weeks if you took care of yourself.

God Works in Mischievous Ways

Consumed with self-pity, I even thought I'd ruined my health forever serving the Lord. I soon became angry with God. "I had worked so hard for him and he let this happen," I told myself. All of the sudden the light, joy, and enthusiasm seemed to evaporate from my life.

Although being a workaholic had contributed to my illness, I initially convinced myself I could work my way out of this funk. I continued working hard—even harder than before and much harder than anyone around me. But I only sank deeper into my depression.

I then tried reasoning my way out of it. I remember sitting on my patio one spring morning and telling myself, "I have a wonderful family, a good church, and many friends. I ought to be happy." But I was not. Nothing I did to get myself out of this dark pit helped. It was if the sun had set on me and would never shine again.

I finally realized I needed help, but I was too proud to go to a psychiatrist. In another one of his mischievous and miraculous ways, God provided for me. A Mennonite medical missionary from Nigeria named John Glass had returned to the States to study psychiatry at the Menninger Clinic in Topeka, Kansas. As a part of his studies, the clinic sent him to San Marcos to do case studies on the young men in the Job Corps Training Center. Since there was no Mennonite church in town, he began attending our church for the few months he was working there.

I had met John at church and learned about why he was living in San Marcos. I called him out of desperation at his home one night and asked if I could see him. In our visit I poured out my life's story to him. After listening for a long while, he said, "Paul, you're the kind of person who gets things done, but you pay a high price for it. This is a part of that price." Then he told me, "If we do nothing, you will come out of this depression in about six months on your own, but I can prescribe something for you that will help you get through it easier."

He must have sensed my resistance to the idea of medication because he then followed with, "If you broke your leg and I could give you a pain pill to relieve your suffering, you wouldn't hesitate to take it, would you?"

I thought for a moment and replied, "No."

"Good," he said as he wrote the prescription on his pad of paper. He tore off the sheet, handed it to me, and said, "This medication is for emotional pain, and it will help the same way."

He cautioned me not to expect immediate results and explained that depression is the result of a chemical imbalance in the body that can be caused by many things—prolonged stress, unresolved anger, or some loss. I had experienced all three. My loss had not been a loved one—I had actually lost "me" somewhere along the way. The depression shattered my ego because I had always prided myself in being strong.

The medicine would restore the chemical imbalance, but it would take a while for its effect to build up in my system. He warned that it could be two or three weeks before I would see improvement. I still had a heavy heart, but for the first time in many months I had a sense of hope.

When I was at the height of my depression I didn't want to go anywhere. I didn't want to see anyone. I didn't even want to visit people in the hospital without Cathy at my side. I just continued to do my work every day at the church without letting on what was going on inside of me. A few weeks after starting the medication we were expected at a banquet in New Braunfels. As usual, I dreaded going out. But in the middle of the event that Thursday evening a glimmer of hope dawned on me: "I'm

God Works in Mischievous Ways

not depressed any more." It wasn't that simple, and I wasn't fully healed, but I was on the road to recovery. After several more months, the doctor slowly began to decrease my medicine and finally weaned me off of it completely. It was still about a year before my depression would be completely behind me, but that night at the banquet marked a new beginning.

After this terrifying ordeal, I understood depression better and could empathize with people who told me about their own similar experiences. People who have unresolved anger at others or God and those who have recently lost a loved one can often fall into depression. Up until my own battle, if a person had come to me saying they were depressed I would have said, "Just snap out of it. Count your many blessings, name them one by one…" But I had tried that strategy myself repeatedly and it didn't work.

It's okay to be angry with God, by the way. He understands, and he can take it. What's not okay is unresolved and sustained anger. It can be devastating to the person who holds it inside. Some people believe that all depression is rooted in anger, and I tend to agree. Holding on to resentment is like holding a lit match. If you hold it long enough, you will be the one who's burned.

When I was in a deep hole, and couldn't climb out by myself, the Lord sent a Mennonite doctor to pull me out. The timing was impeccable. I left San Marcos a few months after the fog had lifted, and a few months after that, the doctor returned to Kansas having completed his work assignment. I have never heard from him since. I believe with all my heart that God sent him to San Marcos at just that time to save my life and ministry. Have I told you? God moves in mischievous ways, his wonders to perform. You'll never convince me that God was not in this for my benefit.

However, I was not completely out of the woods yet. Depression can often linger long after you think it's finally gone away. I left San Marcos after serving six years there to be the pastor of Green Acres Baptist Church in Tyler, Texas. With a booming population of 57,000, Tyler was the queen city of East Texas. The largest church in town was First Baptist, with an average attendance of more than 1,300 in Sunday school. Green Acres averaged more than 700 when I became their pastor in 1972. Although it would prove to be the greatest pastorate of my life, after the excitement of the initial move to Tyler wore off I was dismayed to find that I was still unhappy. I made a quiet plan to quit and even get out of the ministry altogether after my first two years at my new job in Tyler. That is, if I could make it that long.

CHAPTER 10

God Has a Plan for His Church

Our mission begins at the ends of our nose and our toes and goes and goes until we have told all men everywhere that Jesus saves.

JUST ABOUT THE TIME I FELT I SHOULD LEAVE SAN MARCOS, TWO PASTOR SEARCH COMMITTEES VISITED ME ON THE SAME DAY. One was Whitesburg Baptist in Huntsville, Alabama, and the other was Green Acres. Huntsville is home to the U.S. Army's Redstone Arsenal and was the center of the U.S. space program during the "race to space" with the Soviet Union. Whitesburg was a great church with an attendance of more than 1,000 in Sunday school. As you might expect with several space program personnel in the church, their search for a pastor was rather scientific-based. The committee had fed the profile they wanted for a pastor into the Southern Baptist Convention church records data bank, and my name was one of the names that the computer spit out. How's that for spiritual direction?

Leo Chesley, the chairman of the Green Acres committee, had slipped quietly into our services the same Sunday that Whitesburg was visiting. He would have slipped out unnoticed after the service too if a photographer had not been standing by the exit taking pictures for our church's pictorial directory. He suddenly grabbed Leo by the arm and said, "Here, shake hands with the pastor and let me get a picture." Before Leo knew it, his picture had been snapped and a record of his visit preserved for posterity. So much for pulpit committees trying to be anonymous.

Both committees called me on Monday morning to set up a time to visit with them. Whitesburg wanted Cathy and me to come to Huntsville, while Green Acres wanted to meet us at Stagecoach Inn in nearby Salado. I told Whitesburg I would visit during my upcoming vacation. In fairness, I then told the Green Acres committee about Huntsville. Undeterred, Leo said, "You need to visit us before you go to Alabama." So we drove to Tyler and met with the entire deacon body at a beautiful lake house. They wanted me to come in view of a call, but I said I wouldn't give them an answer until I had visited with Huntsville. I was not playing one against the other; I was just trying to play fair. Cathy and I flew to Huntsville and halfway through the interview I knew this was not the place for me. Don't ask me how I knew; I just knew. Huntsville was a good deal larger than Green Acres, but it wasn't where I belonged.

This wasn't the first time a Green Acres pulpit committee had crossed paths with me. Many years earlier I had preached a revival at First Baptist Rockdale. On Sunday morning Judge Connally McKay and his wife, Glee, were on their way to a judicial meeting in Austin and stopped to attend the church service in Rockdale. Green Acres was looking for a pastor then, so the McKays told the committee about me after they returned to Tyler. However, the committee never called. Years later Judge McKay told me that committee held two strikes against me. One, they felt that I was too young then, and they were right. Second, in a strange coincidence another church in Tyler had had a preacher also named Paul Powell who had recently moved away. They assumed he was the same Paul Powell that Judge McKay was talking about and promptly dismissed me as a candidate!

After this new committee at Green Acres invited me to preach, the church voted me to be their pastor. I felt I needed to leave San Marcos for all the reasons I described earlier, but on the other hand I was not sure I was ready to leave. I asked Leo to give me a week to pray about accepting their invitation. By the end of the week I was still undecided. Leo called again and I asked for another week extension. I didn't want to leave my friends in San Marcos, but I needed to go. I was in such agony one day that I prostrated myself on the floor of my study to seek what God wanted me to do. I had read in the Bible about people in great distress prostrating themselves before the Lord, so it seemed like a good idea. Lying there I said, "Lord, I don't know what to do."

Nothing.

Then I said, "Lord, I am going to Tyler if you don't throw up a roadblock that a blind man can see."

Still nothing.

Finally I said, "Lord, I'm not threatening you, but I am going if you don't stop me."

I still didn't hear anything, and I eventually got up and went on with my day.

The next day I received a telephone call from the president of the largest savings and loan in San Marcos asking me to come see him. He had obviously known I was considering leaving and asked, "Paul, what would it take to get you to stay in San Marcos?"

"All I want to do is God's will," I told him.

He responded, "Suppose we build you a new home?"

Cathy and I had never lived in a home of our own. We'd always lived in parsonages—one-size-fits-all homes owned by the church.

"No, I just want to do what is right," I said, bringing the conversation to a close without bringing me any closer to a decision.

I walked away from his office wondering, "Lord, is that the roadblock I asked for?"

I quickly dismissed the idea because I was convinced that's not the way God works. I remembered Jesus' temptation in the wilderness to fall down and worship the devil in return for all the kingdoms of the world. God doesn't bribe us; he simply presents choices.

Although I still had my reservations about leaving, we finally accepted the call at Green Acres. However, the next "call" I received before I left San Marcos was the anonymous kind.

When I answered the phone in my study, an unidentified voice blurted out, "Are you going to Tyler?" He had not bothered to introduce himself.

Curious, I replied I was in fact going to Tyler and was about to ask his name when he quickly said, "Watch out for…" (He named a man's name.) "He is a vampire and will eat your guts out."

"Who is this?" I asked. And with that there was a click on the other end of the line.

You don't quickly forget a call like that, so I tucked the information into the corner of my mind. We moved to Tyler and lived in a rented apartment while we built our first home.

My friends in San Marcos knew the difficulty I had in making the decision to leave. Almost every week I received a telephone call or a letter from someone saying that I should come back to San Marcos where I "belonged." My best friend, Ronnie Wilson, was chairman of the pulpit committee that San Marcos assembled after I left. Every call he made asking me to come back made me more homesick and my life more miserable.

Early in December, just a few weeks before our new home was to be completed, I announced to Cathy, "I'm going back to San Marcos."

My good wife usually knew God's will for us before I did. All of the churches where we served would agree that she was the ideal pastor's wife—especially for me. Cathy and I share the same values on every front. She had never tried to influence me in my decisions, but this time she urged me not to consider going back to San Marcos. I should have listened to her, but I was determined to try to go back anyway.

My conversation with Cathy took place on a Wednesday afternoon. I then made several calls to Ronnie before and after the prayer meeting that evening to tell him I was ready to come back. However, I was never able to reach him.

When I finally reached him Thursday morning, he quietly listened before he said, "Oh, Paul. We met last night and invited a pastor to come in view of a call."

I hung up the phone and thought to myself, "There was the roadblock." It was not to keep me from going but to keep me from going back. From that day on I settled down and had peace about being in Tyler. If I had gone back to San Marcos, it would have been the biggest mistake of my ministry. I've said it already, but I need to say it again, "God moves in mischievous ways..."

***

One reason Green Acres has always been a good church is because it was born well. Porter Bailes, the pastor of the First

Baptist Church in Tyler, was a strong leader who sensed discontent in some of his younger members. He encouraged them to organize a new church and even allowed them to meet in the basement of First Baptist and call their first pastor. In the meantime he led First Baptist to buy five acres of land in what was then South Tyler to begin the first unit of a church building. By the time this fledgling congregation moved in, they had 250 members and were self-supporting. Some of the good people of First Baptist went with these pioneers to help establish the church and later returned to the mother church. By the time I became pastor at Green Acres, the church was 17 years old.

I remember sharing my reservations with Dr. Charles McLaughlin, who was then the director of the State Missions Commission of the Baptist General Convention of Texas and had served as interim pastor of Green Acres three times. Up to that point I had always pastored one of the largest churches in smaller towns. In Tyler I thought I would be just another one of many pastors. "I'm not sure how I'll like being a little fish in a big pond," I admitted. He just smiled and assured me that I wouldn't be a little fish at Green Acres for long. He did not know me—he just knew Green Acres' spirit and its potential.

One of the things that impressed me about the people of Green Acres was the way they sang from their hearts with gusto. I noticed this on my first visit there before I'd agreed to become their pastor. I was also intrigued that they filled up the church from the front to the back. It's hard to explain the chemistry between a pastor and his people, but it's the same with a shepherd and his sheep. We formed an almost instantaneous bond and went after more people together.

Early in my ministry I learned the difference between leadership and management, but I did not know what to call it. When I read a biography about President Andrew Jackson, I realized I had what is called an executive temperament, not an administrative one. Like me, Jackson had little patience for endless meetings where little gets decided. He actually resigned from Congress because he was too much of a man of action.

One of the first things I did after becoming pastor at Green Acres was to lead the church to call Dennis Parrott as minister of education. During his first few weeks I learned Dennis had an administrative temperament. I told him I also wanted him to serve as the administrator of the church, which he agreed to do. He had hardly left my office when I picked up the phone and asked a lady I knew to direct our first all-church picnic.

As soon as Dennis heard about this he was back in my office asking, "Do you want me to be the administrator or not?"

I said I did.

He responded, "Then leave this picnic alone and let me do my job."

He and I were a good team. I was learning how to let go—another key to good leadership.

I began my ministry at Green Acres with a bold, clear vision of being the greatest evangelistic church in East Texas. I was not trying to be better than everybody else. I simply wanted us to be our best and if we did that, we would be the greatest. The first thing Dennis and I did was visit prospects. That's the best way to begin any new ministry. We visited every newcomer in Tyler, and I made a special visit to every person who visited our church. I often said from the pulpit, "If you would like a visit from the pastor, indicate it on the card. I can't visit everyone, but I sure can visit you." People appreciated that we tried to bring a personal touch to our ministry even after folks began to join in large numbers and the church began growing.

Our initial success led to jealousy on the part of some of my fellow pastors. I remember one of them saying, "You just happened to be in the right place at the right time." I admit it does help to be in the right place at the right time, and it was a good time in my life for a challenge. Bu there's a lot more to it than that.

To prove my point, I often point to our location. I explain that Green Acres was located on the north side of a large shopping center in South Tyler. Directly across the street south of that shopping center was a church of another denomination. The two churches had a lot of similarities. They were the same age, located in the same part of the city, preached from the same Bible, and had access to the same prospects. But while we blossomed and grew, the other church actually declined. Part of the secret to our success was that we had an unabashed commitment to growth and we worked like the dickens.

At the end of my first year I had a showdown with the deacons over leadership. After I returned with a group of young people on a mission trip to Belize, the youth were on fire for the Lord. They wanted to serve the Lord's Supper on that Sunday night so I asked and received permission from the chairman of the deacons to do so. At the conclusion of the service I left town on vacation, and the deacons had their regular monthly meeting. I later heard that two of the deacons didn't like the way we'd conducted the service. In a bold move, these two men then asked the other staff members in the meeting to leave the room so they could talk about us! The chairman of deacons should have spoken up and explained that I had asked him for permission. But he said nothing in my defense. I was beyond angry.

When I returned home, I immediately met with the men who had asked my staff to leave the room. I reminded them that even in the business world people have the courage to look one another in the eye and say what they have to say. I told them, "If anybody suggests asking the staff to leave the room so they can talk about them, I expect you to stand to your feet and say that we don't operate like that around here."

I then called all of the deacons together and said, "You have been talking about me. Now talk to me."

There was a long silence.

Finally, I said, "What happened here the other night will never happen again. I have appointed [I named one of the men from my earlier meeting] to see to that." I looked at him and said, "Isn't that right?"

He spoke up and said, "Yes, that's right."

I then reminded them how they'd already had three pastors in the young life of the church. I said, "If a man comes to me and says to me, 'I've been married three times and I'm now having trouble with my fourth wife,' I get the idea that the problem is not the wife but the man."

I finished off my speech with an ultimatum: "You folks have a problem. Now we can square off and fight, or we can be friends. But I am going to be the leader of this church if I stay."

After a minute my friend Leo said, "Pastor, would you mind leaving the room?"

I did not mind leaving them to let this sink in and informed them I would be at the tennis courts if they needed me. This time, they weren't asking me to leave because they wanted to talk about me; they actually voted that night to give me a gift for my first anniversary. That was the night I became the leader of the church.

God Works in Mischievous Ways

CHAPTER 11

All Healthy Churches Grow

*There are two kinds of pain in a church:
growing pains and dying pains.
Growing pains are better.*

I KNEW I WAS SKATING ON THIN ICE, BUT I HAD TO GET THE CHURCH OUT FROM UNDER THE THUMB OF THE DEACON BODY IF IT WAS GOING TO PROSPER. When one of the men leading that painful episode died a few years later, his wife gave me his beautiful tiger's eye gold ring that I have worn for more than 35 years. It is a daily reminder to me that it's possible to have conflicts with people and still remain friends.

In time we ran out of space to hold all the families who were coming to Green Acres, and by then I had forgotten all about quitting the ministry. My depression in San Marcos had been triggered by circumstances, and when my circumstances changed I got better. This is just one reason among many why Green Acres was a turning point in my life and ministry. We had so many visitors that we began hosting a fellowship just for guests after church. I wanted to meet everyone personally and thank each one for coming to church that day.

We were growing exponentially and I initially tried to maintain the momentum with special gatherings. We featured special guests like Paul Anderson, "The World's Strongest Man," and Tom Lester, one of the stars from the 1960s television show *Green Acres*. We even had Norma Zimmerman from the old *Lawrence Welk* variety show. But Green Acres was unusual. They were not necessarily impressed with celebrity; they seemed happier to hear God's Word preached Sunday after Sunday.

Periodically, younger preachers will contact me about my sermon preparation. For example, they want to know if I preach without notes. I did so until I came to Green Acres where I had so many preaching engagements that I could hardly memorize every sermon. But I never forgot what Will Rogers said: "If a preacher can't remember his sermon, how does he expect me to?" Pressure and time constraints became greater than I could handle, so I developed a scant outline with names, keywords, and dates and preached from that.

My preaching style developed over time throughout my ministry, but I settled into an effective pattern. First, I would develop a thesis—a one-sentence summary of what I wanted to say. Then I would break the thesis into bite-sized chunks that I called the points of the sermon. After I wrote an attention-getting introduction, I would state my thesis, followed by the points I wanted to make. I thought of the thesis as a nail—a single truth I wanted to drive into the hearts of my audience. The points of the sermon were like the blows of a hammer, each one driving the truth deeper into the hearts of my hearers. After each point I would go back and restate each one.

I kept the sermon moving rapidly from one point to the next. We live in an impatient world. Most people speak at a rate of 100–150 words per minute. But people can process 500 words a minute, leaving a lot of lag time for their minds to wander. To put it another way, we can hear approximately four times faster than anyone can speak. I was reminded of this truth when I conducted the funeral service of Judge William M. Steger, a federal judge for the Eastern District of Texas. In his 35 years on the bench, he worked more than 15,000 cases. Judge Steger was also a genuine American hero. In World War II he flew 56 combat missions, returning after one mission to his base in North Africa with 96 bullet holes in his plane.

He had very little patience for ill-prepared attorneys who would dilly-dally in his court. He often said to them, "Have a point. Make your point. Then move on." Long before I preached the judge's funeral, I had adopted that same method of preaching. It's not only good advice for lawyers, it's also good advice for preachers and anyone trying to persuade people to a certain way of thinking. In fact, preachers and lawyers both have a similar purpose: to build a case so as to win a verdict. The good judge's advice applies to the pulpit as well as to the bench: have a point, make your point, and move on.

I once read about a young Methodist minister in his first pastorate who received a visit from the bishop one Sunday. Naturally, the young minister was very nervous to host this special guest during the service. When it was over, he asked the bishop, "Will that do?"

"Do what?" replied the bishop.

When people don't know what you want them to do, you have missed the point. In seminary I remember having to deliver a sermon to the class for the first time. I was as anxious as I could be, knowing the students and my professor would grade me afterward. As usual, my grade that day was average. I'm not a flashy preacher. I've always sought to speak in a simple, straightforward manner so that the last and least person in our congregation could understand me. When I left Green Acres, the third-grade choir wrote me some letters I have always treasured. One child wrote, "Thank you for being our preacher. Thank you for making the sermons interesting. And a lot of times I knew what you were talking about." I have an idea some deacon wrote that and signed a kid's name to it. But the fact remains that no one young or old ever had trouble understanding what I was saying.

I think people are fed up with not being fed in church. I remember a young mother of three visited our church one Sunday. When I called her later that afternoon to follow up, she remarked how much she enjoyed hearing God's Word preached. Raised a Methodist, she asked me, "Do you preach from the Bible often?"

I smiled to myself and said, "Every Sunday."

"Oh, I need that," she responded.

Everyone needs that, and it's the preacher's job to give it. Sheep like to be fed; they never resist. When they are fed repeatedly, they will follow their shepherd where he leads them. God's Word, the Bible, is the original soul food. I always tell pastors to make sure their sermons are clearly from God's Word. After all, that's what people want and need—a Word from God. And that's all we have to say. Everything else is illustration and application.

This is why I always started my sermons with the text, calling the people's attention by saying, "Open your Bibles to…" Then I would use a bit of humor while I waited for them to find the chapter and verse. I always came quickly to the scripture because I wanted people to know that what I have to say is based on

God's Word. At the end of every sermon, I always closed with a strong evangelistic appeal—always. I wanted to see people saved. I followed the rule of Communication 101—tell 'em what you're going to tell 'em; tell 'em; then tell 'em what you told 'em.

I'm often asked about where I get my illustrations. I find them everywhere: in the newspaper, magazines, television programs, general reading, and in listening to other speakers. Of course, in the ministry you gather a lot of illustrations just by being around people. I tell pastors to pay attention to people. They will give you stories and ideas that spark whole sermons. "After all," I say, "you're preaching to people, not to pews." I filed all my illustrations by subject in manila folders, but of course you can scan and file them on computers too. I consider illustrations the windows that let in the light and the fresh air. I have archived my sermons almost from the beginning of my ministry. I figured if I was going to spend a lot of time studying and preparing for it, I should save the material for future use. If a sermon is worth preaching once, it is worth preaching twice. Of course some of mine weren't worth preaching once, but I did it anyway. And God continued to grow his church.

A seminary student once sent me 10 questions in an email regarding the role of the pastor. Instead of doing his homework for him, I simply wrote back the same advice I give to all young pastors: preach the Word, love the people, and lead the church.

Preaching is, of course, primary. Love for the people is a given. Pastors must ensure their people have no doubts about that, and they must learn to love them in a variety of ways. It's true that people don't care how much you know until they know how much you care. Biblical leadership grows from love for the people and from their love for you. They may follow a leader out of fear, but it is far better for them to follow because they know he or she loves them.

The third responsibility of the pastor is to lead the church. When the pastor leads the church, the staff and people follow. If

I had to pick one common weakness among preachers, it would be that most of them are far too passive. Nothing ever rises above the leadership. People prefer doing nothing instead of doing something. That's not unusual—it's just human nature. It's no wonder people need leaders. The 23rd Psalm describes the ideal shepherd as one who carefully guides the sheep and leads them right where they need to be. Leadership is a vital part of the shepherd's responsibility, and it has its ups and downs. We need to stay the course if we are going to grow God's church.

***

We soon needed to build a children's building at Green Acres, but the church was landlocked between shopping centers on the north and south, coupled with a neighborhood to the west and a road to the east. The subdivision restrictions near the church required that the houses remain single-family dwellings for the first 25 years. That was still a long way off. The only available land was a drive-in hamburger stand on a side street across from the sanctuary. It wouldn't be safe to put children across the street, so we decided on something else instead. We would build a Family Life Center first to minister to families through recreation.

That plan, like a lot of other innovative ideas we had, initially met with opposition. First, it was a lot of money for the church. When I announced from the pulpit that it would take more than a million dollars to build the Family Life Center, a friend of mine told me that he nearly fell out of the upstairs balcony! He did not think we could raise that kind of money. But I knew we could.

Dennis and I suggested to the building committee that we hire a financial firm to help us raise the $1,200,000 we needed. Some of the best leaders in the community comprised the committee. When we suggested an outside fundraising firm, one man insisted we could raise the money by ourselves.

I was not convinced so I asked him, "How much do you think an advanced gift ought to be?"

He thought for a moment and suggested $5,000.

I told him, "If you aren't thinking any bigger than that, we might as well close up shop and go home. I intend to give more than that, and I'm sure you're going to out-give me."

They decided to hire the firm.

Another challenge we encountered with the Family Life Center was explaining to people how God could use something like recreation as a ministry to reach new people. One day a man came to my office to express his opposition, suggesting that we should give the money to missions instead and not spend it on ourselves. He had it all wrong, I explained. We could raise more money for a building we were going to use every week than for anything else. I wanted to help him see the potential this building had for extending our reach for the kingdom, and that included missions. "If you're going to shoot off a Roman candle, you can do it from a city park," I continued. "But if you're going to send a missile to the moon, you need a strong foundation. We're in the business of sending gospel missiles around the world, and we need a solid base. If you will help me build this building, I promise you that we will eventually do far more for missions than a million dollars would ever do."

I wasn't sure he was convinced, so I added, "If you are still in opposition when the time comes to vote on this, I hope you will stand up and express your feelings." Sure enough, on the night of the vote to build the Family Life Center he was the only one who voted against it. To his credit he made a financial pledge anyway, and when his work took him to another city he came by my office and paid his pledge in full. That's the kind of opposition a pastor can live with.

The Family Life Center became a showplace for recreation ministry—a new concept for churches in the early 1970s. Many churches had gymnasiums, but we offered racquetball, bowling, a running track, games and crafts rooms, and educational space. I've always been committed to church recreation because it's the reason I started going to church in Port Arthur. I knew there were lots of people just like me who would take their first step to the church and to the Lord through recreation. Once people are involved in a sport, it is a shorter step for them to visit the church where their other team members attend.

Our recreational ministry at Green Acres was outstanding, far exceeding my expectations. At one time we had 13 softball teams in the city/church league. Fifty basketball teams played in our own intramural league. One year both our men's and women's softball teams won the state championship, and the next year our boys won the state softball championship. I used to joke that we were not much spiritually but we were sure a bunch of healthy devils.

Once again that old green-eyed monster reared its head. Some people began to call Green Acres the "country club church." "If that were true," I thought, "may the Lord give us more country clubs!" We were now reaching people by the droves. We averaged 13 new members joining the church every Sunday for the 17 years I was pastor at Green Acres. That's some kind of growth and just shows how the Spirit was already at work before I got there, and he is still working today.

I've been fortunate to be in good churches from the first to the last. As I've said, all of them had strong lay leaders who encouraged me and helped me to be a better minister. I had learned early on in my ministry to make sure that they knew how much I appreciated them by bragging on them and thanking them for all they did.

The Family Life Center was the first of four buildings we

would construct during my pastorate. We called the building programs "Together We Build," and our folks began to jokingly refer to them as "Forever We Build." Some of our greatest periods of growth came during a building program. Many people assume raising money will scare off prospects in a church. Not so. When a church is unified and building momentum toward a bright future, others join in greater in numbers to be part of the excitement. The more we built at Green Acres, the more we grew.

Word soon spread throughout the Tyler community about how much money we had raised during our building campaigns. I heard a story about a local business club for East Texas oilmen that needed to be renovated at the proposed cost of a million dollars. Apparently, many at the planning meeting were hesitant that they could raise that much. Then someone else remarked, "Green Acres could raise that in a day." That wasn't exactly true, but it made me proud of how generous our people were.

Churches can also reach crisis points over new buildings. At Troy my first crisis came over a much-needed education building. When it was nearing completion we realized we had made no provision to furnish the building. In a deacons' meeting I presented three options. (Not just two choices as I did with the Belfalls tabernacle!) I said we could take the money from our budget surplus, we could have another pledge campaign for the furnishings, or we could leave the building unused.

Our deacons discussed each option at length but in the end took no action. We left the deacons' meeting and went to the evening worship service, followed by our monthly church conference. The chairman of our building committee resumed the issue with our congregation. I asked him to share the three options I had just presented to our deacons. One of the men in the church immediately cut to the chase. He stood and said, "This is a no brainer. If we have a budget surplus, I move we take the money from it, buy the chairs, and start using the building immediately."

Someone seconded the motion and it passed without dissent.

Afterward, I stood at the back door to greet our people as they left. One of our deacons stopped, looked me in the eye, and said angrily, "We might as well not have any deacons around here. It looks like you are going to do what you want to do anyhow."

My stomach lurched. Not only was he a deacon but his father was a deacon, his brother-in-law was a deacon, his uncle was a deacon, and his father-in-law had been chairman of the deacons for more than 20 years.

I hardly slept that night, certain my ministry had come to a swift end. However, I've since learned that perhaps the most common saying in the Bible is, "And it came to pass..." After a few days my friend cooled off and it came to pass. And we bought the chairs.

Leaders with executive temperaments are often ill suited for committee meetings. One of the ways I was able to survive four building programs and help our church continue to thrive was not to enmesh myself in the building projects. I did not go to committee meetings at Green Acres. Sitting around chewing on ideas and never getting anything done was not for me. What did I care what color they wanted to paint the walls? Instead, I made one brief appearance at the onset of a building project to tell the committee two things. "Think big. And call me if you need me."

They never called.

Ultimately, the committee members did a better job than I ever could have hoped to do. This left me free to do what God called me to do—visiting prospects and church members and preaching the gospel. Committees need guidance and Dennis did a masterful job guiding them in the decision-making process. The finest businesspeople may run a bank or a law office, but they cannot effectively lead the church. They can advise, affirm, and evaluate, but they cannot lead because the leader of the church must be on site full time in order to get the full perspective on every challenge and opportunity.

Our last building program while I was pastor involved a commitment to two projects at once. The current sanctuary seated approximately 1,200 people, and we held three worship services. Instead of building a new sanctuary, we decided to extend the side walls of the existing one to double the seating capacity. As soon as we completed that project, we began a new adult education building.

My friend Judge McKay was now chairman of these two projects. When he took me to lunch one day, I assumed he wanted to talk about the buildings. Instead, he asked me a surprising question.

"The committee wants to know just one thing," he said. "Are you going to stay as our pastor?"

There was a time when I wouldn't have known how to answer that question. My initial plan when I arrived in Tyler was to leave the ministry and maybe get a job selling used cars. But we were miles down the road now, and it was easy for me to respond to his question. I said I would always try to do what I felt was God's will, but I promised him that I would stay until the buildings were paid for.

When the buildings were finally paid off, it was my turn to take him to lunch. I reminded him I had kept my word. When the time eventually came for me to leave Green Acres, we would be totally debt free. A friend of mine once introduced me at an event by saying, "When Paul dies I want to preach his funeral. I already have the text, Luke 16:22, which reads, 'And it came to pass that the beggar died…'"

Everything was not peaches and cream at the church—and neither is it that way in real life. The church is not immune to the same kind of work-related disagreements that everyone experiences at their jobs. Green Acres had a longstanding policy of sending each staff member on a mini-vacation on the occasion of every fifth anniversary. The policy had worked well until my 15th year at the church. The country was in a general recession at the time, but our church was prospering as never before. People were continuing to join, and receipts far exceeded our budget.

As my anniversary approached, one of the deacons contested giving me $1,500 for a trip with my family as an unnecessary bonus. One or two others soon joined in expressing opposition. The vast majority of our men, as is usually the case in churches, sat without making any response. When the vote was taken, it easily passed in favor of sending my wife and me on the mini-vacation. But by that time I was livid.

I thanked the group for their generosity before adding, "Baylor has a Seiko watch with the Baylor emblem embossed on it that costs $200. I will buy that watch as a 15th anniversary gift, and the other $1,300 will be in the offering plate Sunday morning. If a gift can't be given enthusiastically, I don't want it." I definitely had their attention. They needed to know that pastors have feelings and self-respect too. No one, not even the deacon body of a church, should be able to push others around.

***

To my knowledge, there is only one person in 50 years of ministry that I could not live with peaceably. I tried and tried, but there was just no way. He happened to be the "vampire" the anonymous caller had warned me about before I moved to Tyler.

He was a deacon, but he never attended meetings unless there

God Works in Mischievous Ways

was a controversy. Then he was eager to come and tell the group what to do! He was well known as a social drinker, even though traditionally our deacons had abstained from the use of alcohol. For the benefit of all of our deacons, the decision was made to appoint a committee to develop a set of written policies. The committee took the recommendation to the deacon body and they approved it, followed by the church's approval. Then a letter was sent to all our deacons informing them of the new guidelines.

Soon after, I received a threatening letter from this man. I folded the letter and picked up the phone to make an appointment to visit with him. In our meeting he accused me of throwing him out of the deacon body, but that simply wasn't true. I recounted the whole process regarding the policies and explained, "These are the policies, and if you want to abide by them, you are welcome. Otherwise, you're excluding yourself. I'm not excluding you."

We parted without resolving the issue. Thereafter for the next 16 years, every time he was in the hospital or there was a crisis in his life, I visited him and ministered to his family. However, every time we were together he brought up the matter. It was a festering wound inside of him.

One day in the 16th year of my pastorate, he came to my study. By this time he was an old man walking with a cane. When he sat down and began to rehash this old issue, I reached over in my files and pulled out the threatening letter he had written me years before. I slid it across the desk and asked him, "Whose signature is on that letter?"

He peered at the letter and replied, "It is mine."

"What is the date on that letter?"

"February 1973."

I said to him, "That was 16 years ago. You've got to let go of this. You have a problem. I don't know what you're going to do about your problem. But I don't have a problem."

With that he jumped up and stormed out of my office as fast as a man with a walking cane can storm. I continued to do my part to live at peace with him. Long after I left Green Acres for the Annuity Board, I made a practice of sending him complimentary copies of my latest books with a nice note written on the flyleaf. I was doing what the Scriptures say, "heaping coals of fire on his head," Romans 12:20. I figured where he was going he needed to get used to the heat.

To my surprise, when his wife died he asked me to return to Tyler and do the funeral. Then when he died a few years later his sons asked me to conduct his funeral service. I couldn't make it because I was in a revival meeting that week, but I would have loved to do it. There are some funerals you just don't want to miss.

CHAPTER 12

Teamwork: It's Never a One-Man Show

Our job as Christians is to take care of the saints…and the ain'ts.

PRIOR TO COMING TO GREEN ACRES I'D DEVELOPED A REPUTATION FOR BEING HARD ON STAFF MEMBERS AND EVEN BEING DIFFICULT TO GET ALONG WITH. That wasn't true from my perspective. I'd always had high expectations of myself, and I expected everyone around me to work as hard as I did. The problem is that I'd never told my staff members in my previous churches exactly what I expected from them. Then I became frustrated and dissatisfied with their performance. This personal flaw did not go unnoticed by others. In fact, one day a friend who knew me well visited my office and said, "Paul, if you ever quit the ministry, don't go into personnel work because you don't know how to pick them." I've eaten crow every way it can be prepared— baked, stewed, barbequed, and fried extra crispy. I don't like it any way it's served. You may gag on it, but it won't kill you. In fact, it sometimes saves your life. When I began serving at Green Acres, I changed my approach.

I let Dennis conduct the first interview with a potential staff member and I conducted the last one. I also made my expectations clear before a new person joined our staff. I remember interviewing the pastor of a small church who was interested in serving as associate pastor. As I outlined my expectations, he listened intently. When he went back to Dennis he said, "You expect a person to work around here, don't you?"

When Dennis nodded, the man said, "I think I'll stay where I am." In one decision, he made us both happy.

I worked under the conviction that the best thing that could happen to a quarterback was to have an all-pro at every position in front of him. The better they did their job, the better he did on the field. As pastor I called the plays, kept the team focused, and motivated everyone to be the best at his or her position. I expected them to stay current with developments in their areas of ministry by visiting other churches, reading, and attending conferences. At our annual extended staff meeting I asked each one to share three ideas other churches were doing in their area that we weren't doing. I wanted to ensure that they were always open to new ideas. It took a while for our staff to learn to work together, but it was the beginning of a fruitful 17-year relationship.

I was demanding of my staff, but I believe I was fair. For example, I expected them to do the basics, including living within their budgets and being at work at 8:30 in the morning regardless of how late they had been out the night before. If I heard complaints, I explained, "If you want to come in at any hour of the morning, go to the bank or a school and see if they will hire you under those conditions." In any working environment team members who straggle in at odd hours soon destroy morale.

I also expected each staff member to visit two prospects a week, visit the hospitals one day a week, perform weddings and funerals if asked, and baptize—as well as take care of their own ministries. I didn't expect anything out of them that I didn't do myself. I averaged about seven prospect visits a week with all my other pastoral responsibilities.

I never let the weather interfere with visiting people. On one of the rare occasions that it snowed in Tyler, I went to see a man I had never before been able to catch. On this day he was home playing in the snow with his son. When I trudged up the driveway in my snow-covered shoes, he was surprised to see me and said, "Preacher, what in the world are you doing out on a day like this?"

I just smiled, shook his hand, and replied, "I'm out because you are in!"

I made a quick contact in the yard and left him to play with his son. He was in church the next week. The worse the weather, the better the visiting because that's when people are always home.

By having some semblance of discipline, and knowing we were all expected to carry our load throughout the week, we built a camaraderie that has lasted through the years. Twenty years after I left Green Acres I received a call from a former staff member thanking me for teaching him how to work—something he had never learned until he became part of our staff.

Although we operated very strategically as a church, another important ministry just sort of happened. We began taking in ministers who had been fired, were burned out, had gone through a divorce, or couldn't find a job. The church offered them a house to stay in and $100 a week until they could get on their feet and find another place of service. I required that they come to our staff meetings and visit prospects to keep them from becoming depressed and feeling sorry for themselves. We always did a lot of talking and laughing in staff meetings, and we became a therapeutic support group for these ministers as they healed from their wounds. Over the years God used this off-the-cuff ministry to salvage the ministry of several wounded ministers. It was one of the most rewarding things we did.

I have tried to be a faithful friend to my fellow ministers whenever they were having problems. I have done this as a pastor, as president of the Annuity Board, and as the dean of Truett Seminary. Sometimes we are hesitant to do that, but my motto is, "When in doubt, reach out." That is what the Scriptures teach. The Apostle Paul said, "Brethren, if a person is overtaken in misconduct or sin of any sort, you who are spiritual—who are responsive to and controlled by the Spirit—should set him right and restore and reinstate him, without any sense of superiority and in all gentleness, keeping an attentive eye on yourself, lest you should be tempted also," Galatians 6:1 (Amplified New Testament). Whenever I have reached out to others in this way, my efforts have always been well received. It's also kept me on my feet morally and may have even saved me from much heartache.

When I led the effort at Truett to restore a controversial Baptist leader to a position of considerable responsibility, some questioned my actions. Some people will always hold something against others, even if God himself has forgiven them. He went through a vetting process in the company of other godly leaders wherein I told him that he "brought a lot of baggage" to the job. "We're going to open the suitcase and rummage through it, no holds barred," I explained. He offered a sincere explanation that he had confessed and received the Lord's forgiveness and was ready to move forward.

Later in private I strongly cautioned him not to disappoint me. "I'd die first," he assured me.

"You won't have to," I said. "I will kill you first."

Throughout my ministry I never met another man who more aptly demonstrated what Christ said in Luke 7:47 after his worshipful encounter with a "sinful woman" at the home of a Pharisee. When the Pharisee objected to her pouring perfume on Jesus and wiping his feet with her hair, Jesus replied, "Therefore, I tell you, her many sins have been forgiven—for she loved much. But he who has been forgiven little loves little." This former pastor loved much.

I knew something about being emotionally spent and depressed, but it took me five years before I had the courage to tell my story from the pulpit at Green Acres. I was not sure how people would respond, but I shared how God had helped me to overcome one of the darkest periods of my life. As I stood at the back door to greet people leaving the church that day, I saw Judge McKay making his way toward me. I wondered what he would think of me now and was relieved when he stopped, shook my hand, and said, "Preacher, you never stood taller than you did today."

Several men who were also strong leaders and businessmen came to my office for a while afterward to say, "Pastor, we never knew anyone else felt that way." And then they would unburden their hearts to me. I learned through that experience that the best preaching sometimes contains an element of confession. When we confess our weaknesses and failures in an appropriate way, people immediately relate because they have them too. What's more difficult to relate to is our glowing successes.

Once again, God was at work in unexpected ways—using the very thing that had bothered me to the point of wanting to quit the ministry to help others who were struggling with the same feelings. It gave me a greater sense of empathy with the Apostle Paul, who talked about an unnamed "thorn in the flesh" that actually served to his benefit and reminded him of Christ's strength in his weakness (2 Corinthians 12:10).

***

With the Lord working so mightily at Green Acres, many young people surrendered their lives to the ministry and went on to serve in some of the largest churches in our state. It may be that the surest sign of a Spirit-filled church is young people committing their lives to Christian service.

On the other hand, I heard some people complain that they couldn't find a parking place near the church. Our Sunday parking began to spill over into the nearby shopping center, and we shuttled people to the church in small buses. The church also began buying up houses around our campus and holding them until the 25-year subdivision restrictions ran out. Before I left Green Acres we had bought 27 houses and lots to use for parking and new buildings.

One Sunday I addressed the inconvenience of parking by saying, "There are dead churches all over this town. You can pull up right at their front door. But if you want to be a part of a church that is growing and dynamic, you may have to inconvenience yourself a bit."

I continued my practice of writing daily articles for the local newspaper, and some of my friends suggested that I ought to write a book. I knew nothing about publishing, but I'd started printing my sermons when I was at San Marcos and they seemed to be well received. I did the same thing at Green Acres. After several years of explosive growth, I decided to try my hand at writing my first book. I got the idea for the title from my friend

Charles Jarvis from San Marcos. He was a dentist-turned-speaker and was billed as "America's Foremost Humorist." He lived up to his billing. Over lunch one day I asked him, "If you were going to preach a sermon, what would you preach about?" He thought for a moment and responded, "I'd preach on 'How to make your church hum.'"

I tucked that away in my mind. When I wrote my manuscript outlining basic church growth principles, I called it *How to Make Your Church Hum*. The Baptist press at the time was Broadman Press, but I did not know anyone there. When Dennis went to a meeting in Nashville, I asked him to give the manuscript to someone there. A few weeks later I received a letter saying they liked the book and wanted to publish it. I was off and running in the book-writing business, and 50 years and 50 books later I'm still trying my hand at it. I am hesitant to say this is my last book. I once asked Russell Dilday, former president of Southwestern Baptist Theological Seminary, "Have you read my last book?" and he replied dryly, "I sure hope so."

I began writing books because I realized that a sermon once given is gone with the wind—no matter how compelling, well delivered, or powerful it is. But the printed page lingers on, and it touches people you may never meet. God himself chose to write a Book. The Bible says in Proverbs that the tongue has the power of life and death, which was good because I always wrote in a straightforward manner like I spoke.

I intended to write only one book, but one book led to another (including some that were translated into other languages). I've given away several hundred thousand free copies of my books as part of my ministry over the years. I remember meeting a preacher named Herschel Ford in college who gave away all of his books. I determined then that if I ever wrote a book, I'd do the same thing. My books somehow always made their journeys to people who needed to read them. One of the first books I wrote was *Why Me, Lord?* about suffering and death. One night I received a call from a man in Canada who had lost a dear friend and was in such despair that he had been contemplating taking his own life. Somehow he came across my book, read it, and had accepted Christ as his Savior. He was just calling me to let me know. That's God again for you—working in ways we cannot imagine and doing the unbelievable.

Eventually there came a point when Dennis and I thought the church was big enough. We were averaging about 1,600 in Sunday school—more than twice what it was when I started. I had a broad-reaching vision from God regarding what we needed to do next, but before we could act on it, I felt we first needed to pay off our remaining debt. We could then use the interest we saved to deepen our focus on missions and begin a dynamic new ministry that would transform the Tyler community for Christ.

CHAPTER 13

Build Something That Will Outlast You

*The church is not a business,
but if it is not run like a business,
it will soon be out of business.*

I HAD LONG FELT WE NEEDED TO MOVE INTO LOCAL MISSION WORK, BUT WHAT I HAD NOT ANTICIPATED WAS GOD BRINGING GREEN ACRES THREE MISSION CHURCHES RIGHT OFF THE BAT BEFORE WE HAD EVEN PAID OFF THE DEBT. His timing is never wrong, so I took this as a sign that we were moving in the right direction.

First, a group of Korean believers asked us to sponsor a Korean mission. Then I learned about a struggling Hispanic church that our local Baptist Association had been sponsoring. The church was having a hard time growing because of a series of mishaps. They had an old church bus they used for outreach, and when it broke down (as it often did), the association had to assemble a group of preachers to decide what to do about it. That often left the bus sitting idle for weeks instead of being used to spread the gospel.

I suggested to our Director of Missions that the association give the Hispanic mission to Green Acres. When the bus needed repairing, I could get somebody to fix it quickly at our expense— which the association eagerly agreed to do. Word must have spread because soon the pastor of Sylvania Baptist Church asked if we would take them as a mission too. This was the church where I'd preached a revival in the 1960s. With a new prime location on Tyler's main loop they had at one time averaged 200 in Sunday school. Unfortunately, they had also endured a series of disagreements and inept pastors, which drove the good people to leave for other churches, including Green Acres. By the time Sylvania came to me, they had only a handful of elderly people, no children, no young people, and no leadership.

I agreed to meet with the church one Sunday afternoon. I told them that I did not have the authority from my church to do so at the time, but I was sure we would take them as a mission under certain conditions. First, they would have to deed the property over to us. We planned to do the repairs on the facility, and if we didn't own it, they might change their minds and want to be an independent church again. Second, the pastor would have to resign. If he had the ability to make the church grow, he would not be calling on us. Third, they would disband their deacon body (which consisted of four negative elderly men). I would appoint a missions committee composed of three members of Green Acres and two members from Sylvania. The committee would make all the decisions so the church would not have anything to fight about. Fourth, when they needed a pastor, I was going to be the pulpit committee. I knew more preachers than all the rest of them put together, and the new pastor would work directly under my leadership anyway. Finally, when they were running 200 in Sunday school, they could become an independent church again. But until then there was no need to ask.

The church was desperate and agreed to all of my conditions. After our deacons endorsed this proposal, it brought Green Acres' total mission churches to three. However, it wasn't long before we added two more. We started an African American church in Tyler and adopted another declining church like Sylvania. Part of my strategy included sending our missions pastor to preach in each new church for a few months until we found a full-time pastor. The full-time mission pastors then became part of my staff and were required to attend our weekly staff meetings and give a report of their work. Green Acres' staff became their support and accountability group, as well as a resource network.

I required that these new pastors make 15 visits to prospective church members every week. What else did they have to do with a church averaging 30–40 in Sunday school? I didn't want them to sit around playing solitaire with the prospect cards. I wanted them out knocking on doors. If they ran out of prospects, I told them to start next door to the church, knock on the first door, and invite the people to church. Then move down the street house to house and door to door until they had made their 15 visits.

Too often larger churches start missions and leave the pastor to fend for himself until he gets discouraged enough to quit. We were determined not to let that happen to these men, and it didn't. All the churches started to grow and blossom, as churches will do if there are enough prospects available and you go after them with enthusiasm. In just a few years Sylvania had built two additional buildings, including a beautiful new sanctuary. Plus, they were averaging nearly 500 in Sunday school.

Another part of my strategy for ensuring the success of mission churches involved our people. Every time we adopted a new mission I would ask a number of our people—teachers, musicians, and tithers—to transfer to the mission church and help it grow. People move overseas as missionaries, and all I was asking them to do was to go across town. They could go for a year or two or a lifetime. They could decide that later.

Once more I saw God's mischievous ways at work when I observed that the more missions we started, and the more people we sent out, the more our own congregation grew. Within a few years of expanding our local mission work, we were averaging 2,500 in Sunday school! Our eight local missions averaged another 700 in Sunday school.

Within a few years we planned occasional high-attendance days where we reached 3,000 in Sunday school. In anticipation of a high-attendance day, I announced I would begin teaching a class in the sanctuary. We advertised it as a nondenominational Bible study open to anyone who wanted to know more about God's Word. I offered to teach through the Bible in a year and promised to take all the fear out of attending Sunday school. I would not call on anyone to pray, read aloud, or answer any questions. They could ask me questions, but I wouldn't ask them anything. On the first Sunday 450 showed up for class, a number that settled over time to a healthy average of 250 people for many years.

***

Being involved in local missions opened the eyes of our people to the needs around them and created a longing in my heart to also provide local food, medical, and dental work. My friend Bruce Brookshire knew we were looking at buying a large trailer to convert into a mobile medical clinic. "Would you let a Presbyterian buy that for the church?" he asked me one day. It was a win-win because he bought the trailer and later became a Baptist!

We set up a doctor's office on one end of the trailer and planned to set up a dental clinic on the other end. Local medical doctors furnished their own equipment, but dental equipment is very expensive and I had no idea where we would get it. One day a traveling salesman stopped by the church office asking for counseling. No one at the church had ever seen him before. I was busy so he went to see Dennis. As they talked, Dennis asked him what he did for a living. The man explained that he sold dental equipment! When Dennis told him what we planned to do with the mobile clinic, a smile settled on the man's face. He had a whole warehouse of used equipment and dental chairs available for our use. Whenever he sold new equipment to a dentist, he took their old equipment as a trade-in. It was all in top shape, just not the latest version of technology. Anything we needed, we could have for free! God was up to his old ways again, and the fully equipped mobile clinic was soon deployed into the community one night a week to provide free medical and dental help. We assisted 1,800 people the first year of operation.

God then gave me a vision of a permanent outreach center in North Tyler where we could do what Jesus clearly commands us to do—heal the sick, feed the hungry, and clothe the poor. We secured a church that had been repossessed by the FSLIC and paid for it in one Sunday. We now had a building and a dream, but we needed additional money to operate the outreach center and feed what I estimated could be 50–60 people daily. Two days after we acquired the building, a man who owned a vending machine business called the church and offered to give us fresh sandwiches since he replaced the ones in his machines more often than legally required.

His offer included enough fresh sandwiches to feed 50–60 people a day—the exact number we'd thought we needed. The owner of a potato chip business and the owner of a local bakery also came forward and offered us free food. When I left Green Acres seven years later, we were feeding 24,000 people a year and clothing 18,000 at our outreach center. The same church building housed the Good Samaritan Baptist Church, another African American congregation. We called a student at Southwestern Baptist Theological Seminary to serve as pastor and within a year he had baptized 57 believers. The congregation had grown to an attendance of exactly 172 in a facility that seated only 171!

God was at work doing what we could never have accomplished on our own. After all, he is "able to do immeasurably more than all we ask or imagine, according to his power that is at work within us," Ephesians 3:20. I had been a pastor for 35 years by this time, and this was the only time anyone offered to give food to our church. God acts most often in response to our faith. Here is a principle of faith I learned through this experience: once we decided, God provided.

As Abraham went up Mt. Moriah to offer his son, Isaac asked him, "Father, where is the sacrifice?"

"My son, God will provide," said Abraham.

And he did—but not until after Abraham built an altar, gathered the wood, and drew back the knife did God provide the sacrificial ram. If you are thinking about stepping out in faith, just know that God doesn't necessarily provide in advance—he provides in response.

***

Now that we had a strong home base, we were also sending "gospel missiles" all around the world in the form of mission work. It was no surprise to me that we became one of the greatest missionary churches in the world. That's how God works.

Every church needs to make a great commotion over the Great Commission, but Green Acres has always been a great missionary church. Without assistance from any other organization, our church built 11 churches in foreign countries (two in Mexico, two in Brazil, and seven in Belize, Central America). I remember being asked to build our first church in Díaz Ordaz, Mexico. It would cost $20,000. Our annual World Mission Offering was now at $100,000, but we usually carried the offering into January with my making pleas for another $5,000 or $10,000 to reach our goal. I decided to add the cost of a church to our regular mission goal the year that we were asked to build one in Mexico. I emphasized to our congregation that we were going to build the church by ourselves. By the third week in December we had already reached our goal plus the cost of that church! Thereafter I added the cost of building a church to our World Mission Offering every year, and we always reached the goal long before the end of December.

We also provided a furnished home for missionaries to use free of charge while they were on furlough, and we operated a children's home in connection with Buckner's Benevolences. With the systematic increase in our gifts to world missions, we were recognized as the largest contributor to the Cooperative Program of any church in the Southern Baptist Convention shortly after I left Green Acres.

Although we had missions in many places around the world, we decided to concentrate on Belize and evangelize the entire country. A local doctor named Kerfoot Walker and other members of our church had been doing medical mission work there for years. Plus, the people of Belize spoke the English language. We took young people to remote villages and conducted Bible schools in the morning with the children. Our college students delivered Bibles, and we hosted tent revival meetings in the community at night in hopes of eventually establishing a church that we would build.

When it was time to build the church, we first sent our building crews there. But that posed a lot of problems. The lumber was off-sized, and it was difficult to get our tools in and out. If it rained all week, it left our crew with nothing to do. It was a big expense in time and effort producing little results. It was time to take another approach. Enter Joe Barrentine.

Joe was a rough and tough housing contractor who was close friends with a friend of mine. My friend told me how much he wished he could get Joe in church, but in the next breath he said this would never happen. Thinking of the upcoming men's fish fry we were hosting, I suggested he invite Joe to be his guest and invite me to go with them so I could get to know Joe. I had never shied away from abrasive men like Joe and Coach Jowers, and I figured I might have a chance to win him to Christ. But at the end of the evening, I wasn't so confident.

Joe agreed to go to the fish fry with us and seemed to enjoy himself. On our way home after the event I suggested we stop for a cup of coffee. I had not yet had a chance to speak to Joe privately, and I was looking for the opportunity. While my friend paid the bill, we stepped outside.

"Joe, I want you to come to church."

His candid response shocked me.

He said, "No, I don't want to go to heaven."

"You don't want to go to heaven? I never heard anybody say that before."

Joe looked me square in the eye and said, "Well, my wife is supposedly going to heaven, and if she's going, I don't want to go."

I shot back, "Well, if you keep going like that you won't have to worry about it. You'll go to hell."

God Works in Mischievous Ways

By then my friend had paid for the coffee and took us home. "So much for that," I thought.

The next Sunday I was on the platform getting ready to preach when I saw a familiar face sitting near the back of the church. It was Joe. The next Sunday after that he was in church again. Thereafter he never missed a Sunday. How could I have known that on the night of the fish fry he was planning to retire from the contractor business and had been feeling bored and lost.

When he left one Sunday, I shook his hand on the way out and asked him to come by my office to visit. He did and I explained to him that we wanted to build several churches in Belize, but our efforts had been stymied thus far. I asked if he would go to Belize, study the situation, and come back and tell me what to do. Joe said he wanted to think about it, but it wasn't long before we booked him a ticket south.

When he returned from Belize, he sat down in my office and said, "I hate your guts."

I had come to expect the unexpected from Joe by now, so I just laughed. "What do you mean?"

"You knew exactly what would happen. When I landed in Belize, I never felt more at home in a place in my life. Preacher, I will give you the next five years of my life."

Five years stretched into 10. During that time Joe made more than 30 trips to Belize, sometimes staying a month or two at a time. He worked with our missionaries down there, but he was in complete control of the building projects. Joe drew the plans, hired local laborers, and supervised the construction. It was just another mysterious way that God worked, using a crotchety retired contractor to build churches in Belize and eventually convincing him to trust his Son as Lord and Savior.

When Joe wasn't working in Belize, I had other work for him to do. Our church owned 18 acres of prime property on beautiful

Lake Tyler. It was a pristine location that never failed to bring Genesis 1:1 to mind. I had a 10-year dream to build a retreat center for our people with a lodge, private cabins, a motel unit, a pavilion, boat docks, walking trails, and a prayer garden. Joe agreed to be the superintendent of the entire job free of charge.

We first built a large open pavilion with a sun deck, picnic tables, and a boat dock. Each year Green Acres hosted an all-church picnic on a Sunday afternoon with as many as 1,500 people in attendance. Families enjoyed playing games, boating, and swimming before sitting down to eat a huge potluck dinner on the grounds. Then they assembled on the grassy hillside leading down to the lakefront for a worship service that included baptism in the sun-warmed water. It was a wonderful time of fellowship and recreation.

By the time Joe was through with the lake property, we had built a beautiful lodge with a 16-bedroom motel unit, a 40-bed dormitory, and three individual cabins. The nicest one with two bedrooms, a sun deck, a fireplace, and a kitchenette was designated as the preacher's cabin, and I was the only one who had a key. By the time Joe finished everything, it was paid for without our ever going to the church and asking for donations. Our people caught the vision for this beautiful property and spontaneously gave extra money to the project.

Our Ministry of Communications began televising our services, and the ratings showed Green Acres having the largest Sunday morning viewing audience of any TV program in East Texas before the Dallas Cowboys came on. (You might remember them—they used to be a professional football team.) I wrote a personal note to every viewer who wrote us, and we worked hard to keep the programming personal and professional.

Green Acres was now one of the largest churches in the

entire Southern Baptist Convention and the largest one outside a metropolitan area like Dallas or Houston. Tyler and Green Acres have always been an anomaly to support such a disproportionately large congregation in a town that then had only 75,000 people. All I can say is that God was at work and leave the explanation up to him.

***

In the spring of my 17th year at Green Acres, God began to prepare me for what was next. I remember very well the day that he once more took me by surprise. He chose another ordinary moment to do something extraordinary. I have never been very mystical, but when I was getting dressed to go to the commencement ceremony at East Texas Baptist University to receive an honorary doctorate degree they were graciously bestowing on me, I sensed God getting my attention. While shaving, I had a profound impression that he had something special for me to do and I needed to get ready for it.

I had no idea what that meant, but I wanted to be prepared for whatever it might be. That moment ushered in another wave of uncertainty and indecisiveness about God's will for my life. His will would eventually lead me along a path to two destinations that I'd never imagined as a young man starting out in the ministry.

God Works in Mischievous Ways

CHAPTER 14

Change Is Part of Life

Don't let the years, and the tears, and the jeers
steal your joy and enthusiasm for life.

I NEVER HAD POLITICAL AMBITIONS, AND I NEVER SOUGHT ANY OFFICE IN OR OUT OF THE DENOMINATION. But I never shunned one either. In 1980 a friend asked if he could nominate me as president of the Baptist General Convention of Texas. I told him I would be honored, but I was not seeking the position. He nominated me in Amarillo, but a native son of Amarillo won that year, and I was elected first vice president. Several years later the same friend asked if he could nominate me again for president. I repeated my mantra that I was not running, but I would be willing to serve if asked. This time the convention would be held in Waco. I didn't realize at the time how much the denominational office was involved in the election of officers, but I soon learned that someone else was their preferred candidate.

When word was out that I was going to be nominated for president, one of the leaders in our convention office called Dennis. In effect, he asked if Dennis could persuade me not to allow my name to be placed in nomination because they were backing another man! If I did so, they would "see to it" that I be elected at a later date.

Dennis knew me well. He responded, "I'll talk to him, but I doubt if he will agree." When Dennis shared the news with me I said, "Not a chance. Leave my name in nomination. I don't play political games." I realized it was an exercise in futility, and sure enough the convention-backed candidate won. I put that experience behind me and focused on preparing my sermon for the next Sunday.

In the meantime I became close friends with Baylor University President Herbert H. Reynolds and was intricately involved in the life and affairs of my alma matter. Through the years Baylor was good to me, bestowing an honorary doctorate on me and presenting me with several other awards. The irony of serving as chairman of the board at a university where I'd once cleaned the floors and toilets to earn enough money to stay in school was not lost on me. I just chalked it up to another example of God being up to his mischievous ways.

One day in 1986 a group of leaders from Baylor including President Reynolds, James Landes, and others asked if they could submit my name again as a candidate to be president of the convention. I once again said I was not seeking the position, but I would be willing to serve if someone else nominated me. By the time of the convention, fellow Tyler pastor Bill Shamburger at First Baptist Tyler had nominated me.

Fundamentalism was on the rise in our convention and was beginning to divide our people. I usually don't like long

God Works in Mischievous Ways

introductions because people aren't interested in all those details
and I already know them. But I did like how Bill introduced me
as "a moderate without an ounce of liberal blood in him and a
conservative without a messiah complex." This time I won handily
and became the president of the Baptist General Convention of
Texas. I called my mom, knowing she would be proud of me. After
I told her the news she said that my dad had always told her, "One
day that boy will be running that thing."

We talked a bit more, and I hung up the phone with my
mom's words still ringing in my ears. I thought to myself, "Dad,
why didn't you ever tell me that?" It would have meant the world
to me to know that my father believed in me. Dad had been dead
several years by then. While he had watched my career from afar,
he'd never once given me a word of encouragement.

My dad became a Christian at the age of 75, just two years
before he died. By that time my parents had moved to a rural
community, and my mother and Pat started walking to a little
nearby church on Sundays. Although Pat could not hear, she heard
the voice of God. Though she could not speak, she said, "yes" to
Jesus. She was saved and was baptized.

When Pat died, my parents were devastated. They'd never
experienced a day without Pat right beside them. My dad told my
mother one day after her death, "If Pat's going to heaven, I want to
go." From then on he was a changed man. What no man could do
in life, my deaf sister did in death. She tendered the heart of a hard
old man toward eternity. God deals with us as gently as he can
and as severely as he must. But he does deal with us. Mom lived
another 25 years after Dad died, reaching her 96th birthday.

Now that I am older, I understand my father better than I
ever did as a young man. I remember talking to him the night
before he died. My mother put him on the phone to speak to

me. We talked just a minute, and before he hung up I told him, "Dad, I love you."

"Son, I love you too," he said for the first time in my life. He died later that same evening.

***

I was still the pastor at Green Acres and was also serving as a trustee at the Annuity Board when Dr. Darold Morgan, the current president, announced his intention to retire. It never entered my mind to run for president of the Annuity Board, nor did I have the slightest desire to replace him. I was a pastor and that's all I ever wanted to be. My desire was to stay at Green Acres until I retired, but I could not deny that defining moment when God had spoken to my heart about being ready for what was next. Looking back, I realize staying on at Green Acres any longer than I did would have probably been a mistake. I figure that by the time I was 65 they would have been chomping at the bit for me to leave so they could get a younger man!

The chairman of the board of trustees of the Annuity Board cornered me one day after a trustee meeting and said, "You need to be the next president of the Annuity Board." In his mind I met all the qualifications. They wanted a well-known pastor of a large church who had some business experience because they managed the retirement accounts of thousands of pastors in the convention. They wanted a pastor because pastors tend to trust pastors, and they understand the needs of fellow pastors. The fact that I had served on the board of the First National Bank of Whitehouse (a small community outside Tyler) was an added bonus.

How a pastor got on a bank board is a story in itself. Bob Rogers, who owned the bank in Whitehouse, was a friend of mine and a member at Green Acres. When I first got to know

Bob we traded stories about each other at lunch. In the course of the conversation I learned that he and his wife had once been members of Sylvania. I told them the story of my dismal revival meeting in 1960 where only one man had made a profession of faith in Christ. Bob smiled and said, "I was that man."

That was the beginning of a rewarding relationship with two of my dearest friends. They owned TCA Cable, a group of 30-plus cable systems scattered over East Texas, Arkansas, and Louisiana. One day he called me to his office and asked me to buy stock in his company at a ridiculously low price. I bought as much as I could afford. After several splits the company sold to a nationwide cable system. You can't always measure results of some endeavors immediately, but that's one revival meeting that paid off in a million and one ways.

Bob then asked me to serve on the board of directors at the Whitehouse bank. Agreeing to serve on a bank board was not an easy decision for me. I kept remembering what Paul told Timothy: "No one serving as a soldier gets involved in civilian affairs," 2 Timothy 2:4. I was afraid that this role might distract me from my primary calling of being a pastor. I even feared that my congregation might frown on it. But it involved only one Saturday morning a month, and I determined that I would learn general principles that could help me to be a better pastor.

Bob was an astute businessman. He kept a sharp pencil, and I learned that one of the first priorities in managing any business is to cut unnecessary expenses. When you cut expenses, you automatically increase the bottom line. I became much better at managing the business affairs of our church as a result. Now it looked as if that prior experience would help prepare me for what God was leading me to do next at the Annuity Board.

The week that the Annuity Board presidential selection

committee met, I was preaching in Ridgecrest Baptist Assembly in North Carolina. They called and asked if I would meet with them for an interview. I agreed to meet them at the end of the week on my way home to Tyler. Jim Plietz, former pastor of Park Cities Baptist Church in Dallas, was on the program with me at Ridgecrest. I shared with him and Carl Bates, pastor of the First Baptist Church of Charlotte, North Carolina, about the decision facing me. They both encouraged me to accept if it was offered to me. The fundamentalist element of our convention was taking over every board and agency and this was, in many eyes, the plum position of them all.

My meeting with the search committee was cloaked in secrecy. Someone met me at the Dallas airport, drove me to the underground parking at the Annuity Board headquarters, took me up the service elevator, and quietly ushered me into a conference room. The only question I remember being asked was, "How do you handle conflict?" By now you know what my answer was.

The next week the chairman called and asked if they could present my name for nomination at the upcoming annual trustees meeting in New Orleans—the home of the New Orleans Baptist Theological Seminary. The board liked holding its summer meeting at one of our educational institutions so members could have a better understanding of the depth of our ministry serving hospitals, universities, children's homes, and the like. I told him I would pray about it and let him know my decision before the meeting.

It was an agonizing two weeks because I didn't want to do it. Leaving Green Acres and going to the Annuity Board was as difficult a decision as coming to Tyler 17 years ago. It seems that I have always had trouble either going or leaving a place—except for Belfalls and Troy when I was a young man. Both of those churches called me the first time they heard me, and to tell the truth I accepted both jobs without even praying about it!

Knowing God's will has never been all that easy for me. Once again my wife seemed to know God's will for us before I did. Cathy thought I should do it. Her concern was my health and well being, not advancing my career. I bought a ticket to New Orleans, but when I was sitting in the Tyler airport getting ready to board the plane, I called the current president and told him I had decided not to accept the position. He urged me to pray about it on my flight down. That request was unnecessary since I always pray on airplanes!

As a courtesy, I met with some of the committee members in New Orleans the next day but shared with them my decision to remain in Tyler. I suppose they sensed some uncertainty in my response because one of them asked, "Paul, what would you do if we elected you anyway?"

"Well, I guess I would pray about it some more." What else could I say?

They then took the recommendation to the full board that afternoon to elect me as president of the Annuity Board. With the understanding that I was not accepting the position, only agreeing to pray further about it, I was elected unanimously as president of the Annuity Board!

Soon the news hit the press, including the Tyler newspaper. I had to make a decision to accept this position or turn it down, and I had to make that decision publicly. My struggle was so intense that I was on my face before God once again. After a time of intense prayer, I made my decision and announced to the congregation Sunday morning that I was staying at Green Acres. They seemed genuinely relieved, and I sincerely appreciated the love they showed me that day. I drove home that afternoon having made my decision, but there was still a frustrating feeling of uneasiness. It was a long time before I went to sleep that night, and I could not reach complete peace.

The next morning in my study I received a telephone call from my boyhood pastor, Brother Wright, now retired and living in Louisiana. No doubt he had heard by the Baptist grapevine about the Annuity Board offering me the position. He then said, "Paul, I was praying for you this morning as I always do, and the Lord gave me a verse for you." He shared Matthew 25:23, "You have been faithful with a few things; I will put you in charge of many things. Come and share your Master's happiness."

"Oh, Brother Wright," I moaned. "Don't tell me that. I turned down the Annuity Board yesterday."

He took the news in stride. "I'm not trying to influence you. I'm just sharing with you a verse the Lord gave me for you today." We finished our conversation, and I hung up the phone more confused than ever.

A few days later I was playing golf with a friend who asked, "How do you feel now that you've made your big decision?"

I stuffed my golf bag into the back of the golf cart with a heavy thump and responded, "Miserable!"

I finished the golf game, went home, called the chairman of the Annuity Board committee, and told him that if they still wanted me I would come. In a scene reminiscent of the time I called San Marcos and told them I wanted to come home, the Annuity Board chairman said they had already dismissed my name and were now looking at other candidates.

The valley of indecision is a very lonely place to walk. You must walk that path alone. You may talk to others, but no one can help you get through it to the other side except the Lord himself. Nevertheless, the chairman told me, he would reconvene the committee and see what they thought about this development. After a telephone conference call with me they reissued the invitation, and I accepted this time.

Chapter 15

Retirement Is for the Birds

I feel like an old tennis ball sometimes. I've been batted around a lot and I've lost much of my bounce. But I'm still in the game.

I MOVED TO DALLAS IMMEDIATELY AND SPENT MY FIRST FEW WEEKS LIVING IN THE HISTORIC STONELEIGH HOTEL ACROSS THE STREET FROM THE ANNUITY BOARD HEADQUARTERS. Cathy wrapped up our affairs in Tyler. I arrived at my fifth-floor office at seven o'clock every morning, and for the first few minutes of every day I would stare out the window watching the city wake up and wonder what I was doing there. Although a brick wall no longer blocked my view, I couldn't help but feel I was that young boy in my apartment in Port Arthur again, staring out at an uncertain future.

I traveled to churches to preach almost every Sunday and talk about the Annuity Board's work. Inevitably, someone would come up to me after the service and say something like, "You don't belong in an office. You belong behind the pulpit." Those comments didn't make my transition any easier. I spent a lot of time alone and a lot more time talking with God. I missed Cathy and my family back in Tyler. I missed Green Acres. But in time I started to feel a little more at home in my new routine. The Scriptures say, "The heart of the king is in the hand of the LORD; he directs it like a watercourse wherever he pleases," Proverbs 21:2. I had to trust the unseen hand of God to know I was in the right place at the right time, and I gradually became convinced that this was God's will for me.

Several years before, I had bought a duplex in Tyler from a real estate friend of mine. Once it occurred to me that I could keep half the duplex for myself and maintain a residence in Tyler, it softened the blow of leaving my middle child, Mike, and his wife, Shawn, who lived in Tyler with our only grandchild, Jordan. Jordan was two years old when I moved to Dallas and we wanted to stay close to him. Once Cathy and I found a suitable home in a Dallas suburb, we often drove over to the Tyler the duplex on Friday afternoons so Jordan could spend the night with his grandparents.

The Annuity Board had assets of 6.5 billion dollars the time, and those assets were growing from new contributions and earnings at the rate of a million dollars a day. I was not a businessman and I knew it, but I had 450 employees including strong business leaders surrounding me who had spent decades in the banking and investment world. Chief Operating Officer Gordon Hopgood had spent 40 years in banking. Chief Financial Officer Harold Richardson had been board treasurer for 30 years. John Jones was in charge of investments. They ran the board, and I related the board's work to churches, pastors, and our denomination. We often said that Gordon was "Mr. Inside" while I was "Mr. Outside."

The Annuity Board was not nearly as well known as the Sunday School Board, the Foreign Mission Board, or the Home Mission Board of the Southern Baptist Convention. So I made it my mission to increase its prominence and get the word out about the tremendous work it was doing to enable ministers to retire comfortably and provide for their families. Most ministers were not knowledgeable about investments and were extremely conservative in their financial approach. We spent a lot of time teaching and training them about investments. Many of them invested heavily in the stock market after they understood more about it, and they increased their returns considerably during the time I was there.

I traveled across the United States meeting with institution heads and preaching in churches, seminaries, and at state conventions. For those nine years on the board, I preached in every US state except three and spoke in numerous countries too. I often joked that I preached everywhere once and one place twice. I began writing a monthly newsletter to all the pastors in the Southern Baptist Convention in order to share vital information about how the Annuity Board could serve their needs. I usually included some teaching ideas and preaching tips. If I gave them something they wanted to read, I figured they might read what else I wanted them to know.

I maintained an open door policy throughout my tenure—and it was not an open door to a closed mind. Any pastor or denomination leader had immediate access to me either in person or by phone. I took all my calls and tried to minister personally to these pastors at the crossroads.

Early on at the first meeting with my executive staff I had

told them, "The only two people I will ever fire are Gordon and Harold, so the rest of you better keep those two happy." Then I started using that sharp pencil idea I had borrowed from Bob Rogers and began cutting expenses. The more money we saved, the more money we had to give to our annuitants. If you don't want to watch the bottom line, don't hire a man who grew up the way I did knowing the value of a dollar!

Perhaps the most significant way we helped ministers during those years was to increase the number of investment options from four to 13. Our insurance department also worked hard at lowering insurance premiums. During my tenure we did not increase health insurance premiums one time. In addition, we had to come up with a plan to address many of our churches' requests for property and casualty insurance. Considering the risks involved in that type of insurance, instead of forming our own company we partnered with Preferred Risk (later GuideOne) to offer this additional service. The management of Preferred Risk saw a niche opportunity to serve ministers and asked me to serve on their board because of my knowledge of church needs. I'll never forget my one-and-only opportunity to play August National Golf Course with their company management—every preacher's dream come true.

The more radical element of the Southern Baptist Convention wanted a "sin-free investment" policy at the Annuity Board. It was already our policy not to invest in any company that was publicly perceived to be involved in alcohol, gambling, tobacco, or pornography. We finally expanded the list to include abortion, but of course there is no abortion industry that sells stock anyway. Still, some people insisted on having this addendum in writing. It changed nothing, but we did it to accommodate them.

In an attempt to reason with them, I repeatedly explained

that the Annuity Board was a fiduciary. A fiduciary is one who manages money for another person. Although many participants in the Annuity Board were ministers, many others worked at hospitals and schools—non-Baptist physicians, nurses, professors, and custodial staff who did not share our Baptist convictions. As a fiduciary, the law required us to manage their money as a reasonable and prudent person would manage his own affairs. In other words, we had to act in the best interest of our participants and not according to our own social convictions. Or else be prepared to face a class-action suit.

Moreover, it was impossible to administer a policy stricter than what we currently had in place without measurably affecting the investment returns. The airplanes in which the Annuity Board committee members flew to meetings sold liquor, and the hotels in which they stayed had bars, cigarette machines, and X-rated movies. Grocery stores sold cigarettes, lottery tickets, all kinds of magazines, beer, and wine. No large portfolio would be complete without government securities, and the government subsidized the tobacco industry. I could keep going with this list of conflicts of interest until there'd be nothing left to invest in but church bonds. Then your only worries would be if the church could remain solvent and pay off its debts—or if the pastor would run off with his secretary.

When the convention met in 1994 in Orlando, Florida, the idea of sin-free investments was looming high. It was rumored that the executive committee was even considering a motion supporting this concept. Some members wanted our investment policy to be monitored by the Ethics and Religious Liberty Commission of the Southern Baptist Convention. Our board had a legal and fiduciary responsibility to control its own affairs, and we weren't about to do that. When I gave my annual report to the convention, I had to set the record straight.

"Since we are in the home of Disney World, I need to tell you that the Annuity Board is not a Mickey Mouse operation, and it is not being run by Goofy and his friends," I said. I left it to the imagination of the messengers to decide who Goofy and his friends were. It really wasn't all that hard to figure out. When I later had lunch with one of the associated leaders of this movement, he suggested I start a sin-free fund because he "might invest some" of his money in it. Maybe some of his money…but certainly not all of it. Even he was smart enough to know that a sin-free policy would be a losing proposition.

God also enabled me to focus on writing books, 15 in all, as part of my ministry at the Annuity Board. They printed the books and gave them as free gifts to ministers at our booth at each convention. Like most people when they hear the word "free," ministers lined up to receive a copy. I would ask them about their annuity and insurance plans and then recommend that they consult with one of our advisers standing nearby. Members of the Annuity Board were on hand, along with insurance experts, to take their questions and help them better prepare for the future. The free books worked so well to draw people in that we translated them into Spanish and Korean and began reaching out to Hispanic and Korean ministers to recruit them into the retirement program.

During this time I was also able to serve several interim pastorates on the weekends, including at Travis Avenue Baptist in Ft. Worth and Park Cities Baptist in Dallas. This gave me the opportunity to do what I do best—preach the Word and love God's people. I felt especially blessed when the First Baptist

Church in Tyler asked me to serve as their interim pastor in 1996 because I could serve a community I loved and be near my grandson every weekend.

By then, Green Acres had called another pastor, Dr. David O. Dykes. I showed him the courtesy of calling him and asking his permission before I accepted being the interim in Tyler. Having been the pastor at Green Acres for 17 years, I did not want my presence to be a problem to him. David is secure in his own skin, and of course it was no problem.

David and his staff have taken Green Acres to places and to heights that I never could have taken them. I felt much like Moses who was allowed to lead the Children of Israel to the border of the Promised Land but was not allowed to take them in. The Lord had already chosen another qualified leader named Joshua to have that privilege.

Little did I know that God was at work in his mysterious ways again. He knew that my daughter-in-law would later be diagnosed with cancer and die when Jordan was just eight years old. Being in Tyler every weekend was a Godsend because it enabled Cathy and me to be close to our family when they needed us most.

My time at the Annuity Board saw years of conflict in one way or another for Southern Baptists, from the rise of the fundamentalists to the retirement of Dr. Herbert H. Reynolds as president of Baylor. When the university was searching for a new president, I was surprised to be among the top candidates for consideration. However, I learned that because I did not have an earned doctorate degree, which some thought necessary, I was eliminated. Perhaps not earning a Ph.D. was the smartest thing I ever did since the next three presidents of Baylor were fired! I would make it to Baylor three years later—not through the door to the president's office but through the servant's entrance as the dean of Baylor's George W. Truett Theological Seminary. Once again, God was working in his own mischievous ways. He knew that everything I ever did in my ministry was in preparation for that next assignment.

When the new president and some of the board members decided they wanted to sell Baylor Hospital in Dallas and funnel more than one billion dollars in assets into the university's endowment, I got caught in the middle because I served on both boards. Pastor George W. Truett had led the First Baptist Church of Dallas in founding Baylor Hospital, and it had been built largely by Dallas contributions. Baylor Hospital had voluntarily allowed the Waco university leaders to name trustees for a number of years as a gesture of goodwill. However, the sudden move by the university board met with strong resistance by the hospital board, and they chose me to chair the negotiating committee made up of representatives of both institutions. This wasn't my first rodeo, and I once again found myself asking God for wisdom to guide each side through a potentially explosive situation.

After a number of meetings, some lasting 11 hours, the negotiating committee settled on a recommendation. It required that 50 million dollars from the hospital be given to the university with the understanding that the hospital would then be free from the university. Everyone on the committee voted for the recommendation except me! I felt that the hospital did not owe the university anything, but I reluctantly agreed so we could settle the issue and move on.

Serving at the Annuity Board also brought me the opportunity to see how other denominations provide for their ministers. Every major denomination has a pension board like the Annuity Board except the Roman Catholics, whose retirement is handled by each diocese. The Methodists have the largest religious pension board in the world, and Southern Baptists are the second largest. (The Methodist pension board is larger because their ministers are required to be in the plan, while Baptist participation is voluntary.) I traveled each year to meet with the heads of these other religious pension boards in order to share ideas and to lobby for revenue neutral bills that would eliminate needless and expensive paperwork required by the federal government.

Because of our size, the Annuity Board was a major contributor to the lobbyists and had considerable influence in these meetings. All the boards paid a lobbyist firm a million dollars a year to represent our interests, and they were accomplishing nothing in my view. I was tired of spending so much money for so little, so I proposed that we not continue to put good money into this effort unless we could see results.

Our leading lobbyist was a fine Christian but was not working the system effectively in my opinion. I raised a few eyebrows when I told the group that I wanted us to hire the most effective lobbying firm available. "I don't care if they drink, cuss, smoke, gamble, or chase women. I just want them to get the job done," I added. I was smiling when I said it, but I was serious. In the end we agreed to hire a new lobbyist firm to represent all of the boards, and within six months the desired legislation had passed. Our new lobbyist was on a first-name basis with senators and congressmen. He wasn't exactly the Sunday school type, but he sure knew his way around Washington and got the job done in a hurry.

I was driving home from the airport after one of these meetings in Canada when I noticed a blur in my left eye. Thinking I was probably just exhausted from the marathon meetings and my demanding travel schedule, I initially ignored it. I later discovered I had suffered a stroke in one of the small blood vessels. My doctor confirmed that my sight in that eye would be permanently impaired. "What if I lost sight in my other eye?" I wondered, fearing I might go blind. I felt old and discouraged that my health had failed when I was busy working for the Lord.

Then I read a biography of Theodore Roosevelt. It explained how the public learned only a year before his death that their president had been totally blind in his left eye for many years. That impairment certainly had not slowed him down. I began researching on the Internet about other leaders who were also blind in one eye. Would you believe the list includes Alexander the Great, Woodrow Wilson, and Wiley Post—the first aviator to fly solo around the world in the 1930s? Not bad for just one good eye. Still, I thought it was probably time to follow through on my plans to retire from the Annuity Board after nine years and fade into the sunset. Yet through another interesting coincidence God revealed that he had other plans in mind for me.

The COO at the Annuity Board informed me one day that he too planned to retire alongside me in 1999 after several decades of service. It did not seem wise for an outgoing president to pick a new COO when I was ready to retire myself. One day Gordon told me that he thought the market was at an all-time high and it had only one way to go. He suggested I might want to retire early while the market was at its peak, so I offered to retire a year early with pay. This would give me some flexibility in planning my retirement and allow them to choose a new president who, in turn, could choose his own staff. The board accepted my proposal, and my official retirement rang in a wonderful Christmas season in December of 1998 when Cathy and I made what I thought was a permanent move back to Tyler where all our friends and Mike and Jordan were. When we left Dallas we would be leaving behind Kent and his wife, along with our daughter, Lori, and her family.

God Works in Mischievous Ways

But Mike and Jordan needed us more at the time. My plan was to sit in my rocking chair on the back porch in Tyler and read presidential biographies.

But I should have known that God doesn't take our plans very seriously. I always liked the story of John Chancellor who, at the age of 67, was just settling into a comfortable retirement after 43 years as a broadcast journalist at the NBC nightly news program when he learned he had stomach cancer. He was bitter and angry before accepting his fate. "If you want to make God laugh," he'd said one time, "tell him your plans."

The first wrench God threw in my plans to retire and do nothing for a while happened shortly before my retirement from the Annuity Board. My longtime friend Bob Rogers died, and I conducted his funeral. He had asked me before his death to serve on the board of the Robert M. Rogers Charitable Foundation that he planned to establish, which I agreed to do. After his death we discovered that the legal work had all been completed, and his will had set aside several million dollars for the foundation. But no one had been appointed to run it.

Shortly after the funeral I met with his widow, Robyn, and his daughter Sherry (the only other board members).

"The first thing we must do is get someone to run the foundation," I said.

They thought for a moment and then Robyn asked, "Could you do it?"

So much for my ride off into the sunset. That would have to wait.

***

A few weeks before I was to retire, I was the new president of the Robert M. Rogers Charitable Foundation. We agreed on a salary, but I told them I wanted to delay the compensation for one year. "If it is doing well, you can pay me the agreed amount. If not, I will do it free," I offered. In the years that followed, this unexpected opportunity gave me the chance to be part of giving millions of dollars to Christian causes, private education, and local philanthropic agencies.

On the first night I was back home in Tyler to stay, leaders from San Antonio's Baptist Child and Family Services asked to have dinner with me. They wanted the Robert M. Rogers Foundation to build a chapel for Breckenridge Village—a residential community for adults with mild to moderate intellectual disabilities.

I had met Bob and Jean Breckenridge and their son Jimmy after church one day many years earlier at the visitor's reception at Green Acres when I was pastor. Jimmy had Down syndrome.

"I bet you don't remember me…" Bob began.

I didn't at first. But Bob knew I was from Port Arthur and reminded me that he had taught me woodshop when I was in school there. Anyone who also hailed from a little town like Port Arthur soon became fast friends. I visited in their home, a small farm on the outskirts of Tyler, and they joined Green Acres.

They were growing older and were concerned about the future care of their son Jimmy. They had offered to give Green Acres their farm if we would establish a home to take care of him and other children like him. They dreamed of creating a faith-based community that would provide care for the "forever children" who needed protection when their families could no longer care for them. There was no way one church could undertake a project like that. However, years later the Baptist Child and Family Services, under the leadership of Kevin Dinnin, worked to make the dream a reality when Breckenridge

Village opened their doors in 1998.

It's amazing how in the wisdom of God things work out. Bob Breckenridge taught me woodshop in Port Arthur and had a mentally challenged son. Bob Rogers had been converted in a revival meeting I had preached in the early 1960s. Now I was president of the Robert M. Rogers Foundation and Breckenridge Village needed help to build a chapel, and the foundation was able to help make that happen. Some people would call that a coincidence. I call it divine providence. The maid of Mrs. Alton Reed was right: "God moves in *mischievous* ways, his wonders to perform."

Sometime after that I was also asked to be on the executive committee of Southside Bank, the largest bank in East Texas. It is a role I still maintain and enjoy today. For the next two years I busied myself with the foundation, the bank, and preaching about 200 times a year from coast to coast. One would think I would be content. However, when I was having lunch one day with Fred Smith, a Christian leader in our community, he asked me how I liked being retired. I surprised myself when I looked at him and heard myself say, "Fred, I need something to run."

CHAPTER 16

God Never Runs Out of Challenges for His Children

*We Baptists have no creed but the Bible,
and I have signed every page of it.
I don't intend to sign anything more,
and I won't sign anything less.*

"IF YOU SAY 'NO,' THAT WILL BE IT. We will never discuss the issue again."

I looked over to Cathy for her response as I was driving on I-20 from Tyler to Dallas to talk with Dr. Robert Sloan, who was then the president of Baylor University. He wanted to talk to me about serving as the dean of George W. Truett Theological Seminary.

She just nodded and smiled, saying nothing in return as I

began to think back on the events that had led to this unexpected meeting. It was now the start of the year 2001. On the heels of my retirement from the Annuity Board, we had moved into a new home in Tyler and had just settled into a comfortable routine. I had no intentions of moving us again—ever—and certainly not to Waco. But I agreed to at least meet with Dr. Sloan about the job.

Baylor University President Dr. Herbert H. Reynolds established Truett Seminary in 1991. Likeminded Baptist leaders such as Dr. Reynolds wanted to establish Truett in part because the fundamentalists had taken over Southwestern Seminary in Ft. Worth. We felt we needed a seminary committed to our historic Baptist principles. As the birthplace of Southwestern Seminary and the alma mater of George W. Truett, Baylor University was the ideal home for the new seminary. It shared its ideal name with the greatest Baptist preacher in our history.

However, the seminary got off to a shaky start. The first class of 50 students in the spring of 1993 received free tuition, and as a result many of those students had not demonstrated the kind of heartfelt commitment to ministry that we wanted graduates to have. Dr. Sloan had served as the first dean of Truett before becoming the president of Baylor University, and the second dean had been fired. The school was now at a crossroads. Whoever became the next dean would inherit a school with some large challenges.

I was serving on the Baylor board again at this time and I, along with others, had recommended a man we considered to be an ideal candidate to serve as the third dean of Truett. However, I learned in a phone call with Dr. Sloan around Christmas of 2000 that our candidate had rejected his offer.

In almost the next breath Dr. Sloan asked, "Would you take it?"

When he said that I thought, "That's like a bride changing her mind at the altar and the minister turning to her maid of honor and asking, 'Will you take him?'"

I laughed and replied, "Robert, I'm no educator. I don't even have an earned doctorate. Besides, I'm retired."

He then asked, "You will pray about it, won't you?"

I think we are supposed to say "yes" to questions like that, so I told him I would pray about it. I didn't take the invitation too seriously because of the objections I'd mentioned. With the Christmas holidays upon us, I gave the situation little thought and did not even mention it to Cathy because I could not imagine God had me in mind for that position.

Shortly after the first of the year, Dr. Sloan contacted me again. This time he asked if I would come to Dallas to meet with him, my friend Dr. Herbert Reynolds (now chancellor of Baylor University), and Baylor board chairman John Wilkerson to talk about my serving as the dean. Cathy had followed me around for all these years, and we were just beginning to enjoy the freedom retirement affords. I wasn't sure I should subject her to upheaval. But when I asked her to consider it, she agreed to go and meet with them.

When we arrived in Dallas for the meeting, I put all my cards on the table and told them that if I served as the dean of Truett Seminary it was going to be a Christ-centered, Bible-based school committed to historic Baptist principles. That was a phrase I would repeat often throughout my tenure to communicate the vision I had for the school.

Dr. Sloan said that was what he wanted, and the others agreed.

I then told them that I didn't know anything about running a school (not the best response when one is interviewing about running a school, but it was the truth). "But," I told them, "if you will give me someone to handle the academics and someone to handle the finances, I can do the rest."

We talked some more and finally adjourned our meeting without my making a firm decision. On the way home to Tyler we drove for a long while before I said anything about the job.

I finally asked Cathy, "What do you think?"

She said without hesitation, "I think you ought to do it."

Once again she seemed to understand God's will before I did. That night I remembered the morning years ago where I'd had the distinct impression that God was preparing me for a greater work and wondered if this was it. Time would tell. With her blessing, I agreed to become the third dean of Truett Seminary in February 2001.

***

The next step in the process involved meeting with the faculty and student body at Truett. The faculty was affirming. The student body was hostile. They tried to intimidate me, but I have been told I can be intimidating also. I later learned that their hostility was part of the reason why the other candidate had turned down the job. The students were seething mad at the administration for what they perceived as the unfair firing of the previous popular dean. Whoever took his place would unfortunately receive the brunt of their anger. In this instance that person happened to be me.

They weren't mad at me—they didn't even know me. After I gave the students a bit of my background, I assured them that we would teach and believe in the inspiration and authority of Scripture and remain consistent with the 1963 Baptist Faith and Message. One of the students then commented, "I thought we were beyond confessions of faith."

I replied with the first thought that came to my mind and said, "A river without banks is a swamp. Truett is not going to be a theological swamp." I then explained that the river was deep and wide. "There's lots of room to row around," I continued, "but we will teach within the riverbanks of Scripture and according to our traditional Baptist beliefs." This was not up for debate, and I told them so.

I came out of that meeting knowing that the first thing I needed to do, and the real reason I think I was asked to come to Truett, was to change the perception of the school and start moving it in the right direction. Fundamentalists were already targeting Baylor, the largest Baptist university in the nation, as a liberal institution of higher learning. It was no surprise that they kept a critical eye focused on Truett.

Most of the existing faculty at Truett were from the East Coast, West Coast, and Midwest. They were talented men and women, but they were unknown to Texas Baptists. The fundamentalists had quickly and broadly labeled these newcomers as "liberal." Since the majority of other people didn't know them, they couldn't defend them. But Texas Baptists knew me, and they knew I was a solid conservative who had led a strong evangelistic church. One of the most important steps I could take, therefore, was to restore Baptist supporters' confidence in the future of Truett.

I immediately began recruiting the best team of men I could find to supplement our already fine faculty. I gave our students access to some of the most widely respected Baptist leaders who could train them to become effective ministers. These men had experience in the field and knew what it would take to equip the young men and women at Truett to reach others for Christ.

I invited Richard Jackson to be an adjunct professor of evangelism. He was the former pastor of a large church in Phoenix, Arizona, called North Phoenix Baptist Church and was a popular conference speaker in Baptist circles. His church had consistently baptized 1,000 people every year. No one could doubt his belief in the Bible.

Next I invited Frank Pollard, the pastor of the First Baptist Church in Jackson, Mississippi, and one of Southern Baptists' most popular preachers. I asked him to join our faculty to teach preaching. I also invited Levi Price, long-time pastor of First Baptist El Paso, to teach pastoral ministry, and Ron Cook, pastor of the First Baptist Church of Brownwood, to direct our doctor of ministries program. David Garland agreed to serve as the associate dean, and I put him in charge of academics. In time, René Maciel (now the president of the Baptist University of the Américas and current president of the Baptist General Convention of Texas) came on board to direct Truett's financial affairs. I was also pleased to hire Joel Gregory in 2005, former pastor of First Baptist Dallas, to teach preaching, and Todd Still, now the dean of Truett, to teach the New Testament. Both men continue to teach there today. We all worked closely together as a good team during my six-and-a-half-year tenure at Truett.

My vision was to position Truett as the premiere Baptist theological seminary in the world. In doing so, we had to establish measurable goals. Under my leadership, Truett gradually increased its enrollment from 150 students when I arrived to 400 students when I left. I knew a lot of people were expecting a lot of me, so I expected more from the students. I requested that every student at Truett serve on the mission field at least once sometime before graduation, and I also developed funding to help them be able to go. Early on, in an effort to further develop more ambassadors for Truett, we also reached out to several hundred active ministers and conferred on them honorary Truett alumni degrees. Many were graduates of Southwestern and felt that their seminary had been "taken away from them" by the fundamentalists. They were eager to be affiliated with Truett. I also began writing a regular newsletter for the seminary and finished the manuscripts of several additional books published by Truett to give away to help promote the seminary around the state, just as I had done when I was at the Annuity Board.

One of the most significant accomplishments involved growing Truett's endowment to 38 million dollars by the time I left. I was able to do this because I knew a lot of the right people, and the people I knew also knew we needed Truett Seminary. Whenever I raised money for Truett in public presentations at churches or various meetings, I often couched my request with humor to put people at ease and challenge them at the same time. I said, "I need two things from you at Truett—prayer and money. If you can only do one, give money. I'll get some old skinflint to pray for us." When people have confidence in the one raising the funds and in the project itself, they are more apt to give. People gave abundantly so that they could be part of the work God was doing.

In consultation with the development department at Baylor, we determined that it would take a minimum of $30,000 to endow a scholarship. I had already determined that I would raise 500 scholarships myself, so I began working toward that goal. I recall how bold I felt when I made my first contact and asked a prominent businessman to give $30,000 for a scholarship.

"You're easy," he said and wrote me a check for two scholarships.

Sometimes we approach a challenge in our own strength and we don't ask in faith. Who knows how many scholarships he would have endowed if I had dreamed a little bigger? There are times to march boldly and times to tiptoe trembling.

On another occasion I had lunch with a very successful man. I asked him to endow a chair at Truett—a gift that at that time would cost one million dollars to cover the salary and benefits of a man or woman to occupy that position at Truett. He politely listened to my presentation, but it was not until I mentioned in a moment of inspiration that he could name the endowed chair after a special friend of his that his eyes lit up. He suddenly stood up from the lunch table, shook my hand, and said, "I'll do it. You just touched my hot button." I learned that he had long been searching for an opportunity to honor this minister who had been a good friend and mentor in his life. God impressed me to connect those dots and bless Truett with a significant financial gift.

I envisioned Truett as a seedbed to grow young pastors from small saplings into well-established pine trees who could stand straight and true for the gospel all around our nation and beyond. We began welcoming 1,500 pastors a year on the Truett campus at various pastoral training conferences, including a general pastor conference, a Hispanic church conference, an African American church conference, a conference for small church pastors, and one for cowboy churches. I wanted these pastors to see Truett for themselves, meet the faculty, and return to their home churches inspired and with a good word about the work God was doing there. In this way we developed 1,500 new student "fishing holes" all over the nation.

We also began a home study certificate program for bi-vocational pastors of small churches who could not attend the seminary campus. Some of these students were not even high school graduates, but they were grateful for this opportunity for a deeper, more structured study of God's Word.

***

I tell you, God moves in mischievous ways. There were so many reasons on paper why I should not have served as dean of Truett Seminary. I was ready to retire. I did not have an earned doctoral degree. I am not a theologian. Frankly, I don't even think

I would have considered someone like me for that position except that the seminary was having an identity crisis at the time. It had developed a reputation for being liberal (which it was not), and they needed a well-known Texas Baptist minister with a reputation for conservatism and church building to help change its image.

That's how God works. You've heard it said that God does not call the qualified but he qualifies the called. It's as true now as it was thousands of years ago when God passed over all of the most qualified men in Israel and chose a shepherd boy to serve as king. As I look back on my tenure at Truett, I believe it was God's will. The man looking back at me in the mirror while shaving that one morning years ago could not have imagined what God had in mind for him. Everything I ever did was in preparation for spending six and a half years of my life helping establish Truett Seminary as the premier Baptist theological seminary of the world.

If there were many excuses for me not to have the job in the first place, there were just as many opportunities for me to bow out early on when things got tough. I recall in the zealous early days of my administration at Truett that I tried to establish a dress code. Truett's campus is unique because it is in the midst of Baylor's campus. Trying to enforce a dress code at a seminary in the midst of a larger college campus that had no dress code to speak of was impossible. The Truett students pushed back and pushed back hard, and I soon dropped that idea like a hot potato. I never mentioned it again, and neither did anyone else. But this incident told me who was really in charge—the students. I had the title, but they had the power.

One of the saddest experiences in my tenure at Truett was to discontinue the scholarship of one of our students who acknowledged that he was a homosexual. In the aftermath of his dismissal, an anonymous email went out to hundreds of people that I had died. For the next few days my friends called Cathy to express their sympathy, and she got a kick out of putting me on the other line!

In November 2001 with almost one year of service under my belt, I came to another crossroads where I could have hung up my hat for good except that God was not finished with me yet. For some time I had felt tension in my throat and behind my neck. I occasionally experienced tingling in my hand as I walked around campus. I mentioned these strange symptoms to my doctor at my annual checkup in the fall, and he dismissed it, saying we would do a stress test later.

A few weeks after my appointment with him, I had a flat tire on a lonely stretch of Highway 6 returning to Waco from a preaching engagement in Stephenville. I worked for at least an hour unsuccessfully attempting to change the tire. I was so exhausted that I ended up calling the Highway Patrol for assistance and then lay down in the grass, my heart pounding. I felt completely wiped out. I remember thinking, "This would be a wonderful time to have a heart attack." Just then a young man came by and changed my tire in five minutes, and I was on my way again. When I arrived home in Waco that evening, I dropped my clothes on the floor and fell in the bed totally drained.

I stubbornly soldiered on with my heavy schedule, which included traveling to preach on Sunday, back to Waco that evening, being in the office Monday, Tuesday, and Wednesday, driving to Tyler for Thursday morning bank meetings at Southside Bank, and taking Fridays off. On Saturday I was on the road again to another preaching engagement. Preaching in churches was important to making the mission of Truett known and raising money to help fulfill that vision. But unbeknown to me I was living on borrowed time.

A couple of weeks after I saw my doctor, a friend and I were driving to Waco on a Friday morning to baptize another friend of mine. I mentioned the lingering tightness in my neck and my friend, who happened to have worked in the medical field, cautioned me not to dismiss it. That week I preached on Sunday in Texas and on Monday in New Orleans. On Tuesday I traveled to preach again in Knoxville, Tennessee. As my host drove me from the airport to the hotel in Knoxville, I mentioned that I hoped the hotel had a shuttle to the airport because I had an early flight out the next day.

He responded, "That won't be a problem to pick you up because I get up at five every morning."

I knew he was a retired minister so I asked, "Why in the world do you get up at five in the morning?"

That's when he told me about his heart surgery and his newfound commitment to exercise. His story prompted me to tell him about the pressure on the back of my neck, and he also urged me to not dismiss it lightly. With these two warnings in mind, I called my doctor from the hotel in Knoxville and asked him to set up a stress test in Tyler the next afternoon on Wednesday. I planned to land in Tyler at 11:00, attend a philanthropy banquet at 12:00, and meet him at the office afterward. At the noon luncheon, on two separate occasions people walked up to me and said, "You sure are looking good." Looks can be deceiving. They had no idea I was leaving there to go for a stress test. But then again I had no idea my life was about to change course either.

After spending about 10 minutes on the treadmill, my doctor stopped the machine. I was sweating profusely, but I offered to go a little longer.

"No," he told me, a serious look on his face. "You don't need to go any longer. What you need is an arteriogram."

He planned to set up the appointment in a few days. However, I told him I had work to do and needed to get back to Waco right away.

"I can't find a cardiologist on a Wednesday afternoon. They're all out playing golf today," he told me.

I happened to be the chairman of the board of the Mother Frances Hospital System at the time, so I boldly ventured, "Well, try."

He did and the best one in the city was available.

Before I went in for the procedure I told my doctor, "Somebody needs to call my wife. She doesn't have any idea where I am. Tell her not to worry and that I'll be home in a little while." Little did I know that no one goes right home for dinner after an arteriogram! They sedated me, inserted a catheter in my femoral artery, and ran a small tube up to my heart where they injected dye to reveal any blockages. They don't even let patients drive for the first few days after this procedure.

When I came to, my wife and a family friend were sitting at my bedside holding a drawing of my heart's arteries. The doctor explained my heart was in good condition but every artery to it was blocked. Two were 95% blocked, two 90%, one 85%, one 80%, one 75%, two 70%, and one 50%. My arteries were so clogged that they were restricting my heart's blood supply.

He said I needed seven bypasses, the maximum number a person can have. I joked that I wanted him to try to do eight so I could make it into the Guinness Book of World Records. But he didn't laugh, and now that I think about it neither did Cathy.

Two days later they were rolling me into surgery. While I was recovering in the hospital post-surgery, my surgeon came by to check on me. He looked at my chart and said with a degree of satisfaction, "I think I bought you 10 more years." That was over 15 years ago at this writing. At the end of my 10 years, I wrote him a note joking that I wanted a new contract or a new doctor.

My family physician knew I loved ice cream and that I enjoyed a bowl of Blue Bell most nights. When he learned about my surgery, he said I would have to give up my ice cream. I said to him, "Doc, I don't smoke, drink, curse, or chase women. Please don't take away my Blue Bell." My earnest plea obviously touched his heart because he replied, "Okay. But just a small bowl."

For a man who felt guilty every time he tried to relax, it was unnerving to realize I couldn't even sit in the front seat of a car, much less drive, for the next six weeks for fear that an accident might break open the wound. I caught up on my reading and finished the manuscript of a book I'd been writing. But I spent the majority of my recovery time burning up the phone lines calling friends and Baylor supporters to ask for gifts to build up the endowment at Truett.

In six weeks I raised more than one million dollars from my recliner. It was a productive time but a difficult one because I felt so much self-imposed pressure to return to campus.

I was back at Truett as soon as possible, and shortly after that we dedicated our new campus. In its early days, Truett met in the First Baptist Church's facilities. Now it was known as the Baugh-Reynolds Campus of Truett Seminary within the greater campus of Baylor University. Long before I had any idea that I would be serving at Truett, I had learned they needed two million dollars to build their chapel on campus. I had suggested that the Rogers Foundation Board give the money and name the chapel in memory of Bob Rogers. The two board members met privately and came back to me insisting that it instead be named after me because of my long association with Baylor University. I was humbled by their request and even more honored when Truett completed construction on the 450-seat chapel.

When Dr. Sloan initially hired me in 2001, he had suggested serving two years. I countered with three years, knowing it would take at least that long to turn the seminary around and begin seeing results. As the end of my third year approached, I told Dr. Sloan I intended to retire as planned.

He said he was not anxious for a change at the helm. I was enjoying my work, so I agreed to stay for another year. I attempted to resign the next year but representatives of my faculty asked me to stay. Truett was an island of calm in a sea of controversy brewing around the administration of Baylor University, and they felt I could keep it that way. It was a time of growing unrest at Baylor, and they looked to me to maintain that measure of stability at Truett. I agreed to stay yet another year. By the sixth year in 2007 life had continued to change, as it always does. John Lily was now serving as president of Baylor University, and I had conducted the funeral of my good friend Dr. Herbert Reynolds, president and then chancellor of Baylor University, in May of that year. Once again I was asked to stay, but after six and a half years I was into my 75th year and felt it was time to go. I recommended that Dr. David Garland be named as my successor. He became the new dean of Truett Seminary, and I was out of a job again.

In the presidential primary of 2008, former New York governor and presidential candidate Rudy Giuliani contacted me through an aide and asked me to be his religious adviser. I weighed his position on abortion and his past marriages and divorces and decided to decline. It would have cast an unfavorable reflection on Truett and on me to accept, but it's an interesting side note to have been asked to the dance.

A year after I completed my service at Baylor, I was named

dean emeritus at Truett. For three years after my retirement
I continued working for Truett raising funds for scholarships
because I believed in the work God was doing there. I headed
home to Tyler to take that final ride off into the sunset, as so many
of my peers and friends by then had done. Yet the sun invariably
came up again the next morning, and I had to figure out what I
was supposed to do next.

God Works in Mischievous Ways

CHAPTER 17

God Saves the Best Sunsets for Last

No church needs to sit around and wonder why they are here or what they are to do. Jesus told us what to do in the Great Commission.

I SPENT THE FIRST TWO YEARS OF MY RETIREMENT FROM TRUETT SERVING AS INTERIM PASTOR OF THE WOODS BAPTIST CHURCH IN TYLER. Then I had the opportunity to serve a second time as the interim pastor at the First Baptist Church of Tyler.

The first time I served as the interim of the First Baptist Church of Tyler in 1996–1997, the church had been in decline and was deeply divided over their future direction. Some members had wanted to relocate. Some wanted to enlarge the present facilities and stay downtown. The church planning committee had been meeting for more than a year but could come to no agreement. After my first meeting with them as their interim pastor, it was evident they were floundering. In the second meeting I took a decisive step and suggested they had met long enough without taking action. "It's time to do something," I challenged them. "The war is going to be over, and you'll still be sitting in a tent." Then I told them a premise on which I had long operated: "I'm going to tell you what to do. If you have a better idea, let's hear it. If you have no idea, let's do it my way."

I then outlined a definitive proposal for them with measurable goals. I proposed that they buy 50 acres of land in the south part of town where Tyler was rapidly expanding and hold the property for future expansion. Then they could devote all their energy to attempting to grow in the downtown location. If they were able to grow the membership, they could sell the land and make a profit. If they weren't able to grow, and they didn't want their church to die, they could build a new facility on the land they had already purchased.

The response of the committee was instant and positive. One of the elderly members who had been a part of every significant decision of the church for the past 50 years was the first to affirm my idea. She then jokingly added, "That's what we need…a benevolent dictator." I was not being a dictator. I was being a leader. There is a difference. You can be aggressive in action without being domineering in your spirit. Think how aggressive the Apostle Paul was with all of the churches—yet no one could question his sincere love for them.

The committee took the recommendation to the church, and it was overwhelmingly adopted by secret ballot vote. Our challenge now was to raise 2.5 million over the next three years to purchase the additional land and refurbish the downtown facilities to attract new members. When we finished the fundraising campaign, we had pledged 3.5 million dollars. Once again I felt like Moses because I was not to be the one to lead them into the Promised Land because God soon called me away to serve at Truett.

However, it should come as no surprise by now that God worked in his unpredictable ways again by allowing me to become the interim pastor at First Baptist Tyler a second time more than 10 years later in 2009. Their search committee had decided to solicit résumés for the position. Someone then consulted the annals of history and recommended me, followed by a phone call from a member of the church staff who almost apologetically asked for my résumé. Before she hung up she warned, "You need to know that some on the search committee think you are too old to serve as the interim pastor."

As requested, I sent them a current résumé and attached my high school picture. I guess they liked the photo because they asked me to take the job. Many years earlier when First Baptist Taylor had hesitated to ask me to be their pastor, it was because I was too young. Now I was too old! Back in Taylor I had sought counsel from Grady Metcalf, the pastor of the First Baptist Church of Temple and another one of my mentors.

"Grady, I hear Taylor is interested in me," I'd said, "but they think I'm too young."

The wise old man had responded, "Paul, if that's your only problem, time will take care of it." He was right. It's been a long time since I've been asked to preach a youth-led revival.

First Baptist Tyler had now accumulated 150 acres of land in South Tyler and had established a second campus separate from the main campus downtown. But the general decline had continued. The south campus offered a contemporary worship style, but they averaged less than 300 in Sunday school. The downtown campus retained a traditional worship style and was averaging less than 500 in Sunday school. For the past five years they had averaged only 75 additions total (and an average of 40 deaths).

I often joked that the south campus was the rock-n-roll church and the downtown campus was the rocking chair church. (One should never try to make a rock-n-roll church out of a rocking chair church, by the way. It won't work.) Out south they had a bunch of racehorses and downtown they were plow horses. Both are perfectly good animals, they just move at a different gait. A racehorse is good for about five minutes. Hook a plow horse up early in the morning, and when the sun is setting he's still at the job.

When I took a closer look at the numbers on my first day on the job, I saw that the south campus had a whopping 40 visitors while the downtown had 50 visitors! I said to the congregation the following week, "You are not a declining church. You are a reclining church." Like many churches that are half full and fully satisfied, they were asleep at the switch and needed to wake up. Jesus said to the church in Sardis, "Wake up! Strengthen what remains and is about to die, for I have not found your deeds complete in the sight of my God," Revelation 3:2.

That week I said to the staff, "We've got a product that people want, but you are not closing the sale." We went to work, following up with visitors and reaching out to the community. The next year we had more than 200 additions to the church! When the prospects are out there, and yet we aren't out there among them, nothing happens. When we get out there and invite people to be a part of what God is doing among families and individuals within the church, people will join because they want to be part of something exciting.

Although their membership had not been increasing significantly, their budget deficit had been growing by leaps and bounds. I was grateful once again that God had helped me learn sound financial management early on so I could develop a plan for getting the church back on their feet—especially as they would have a new pastor someday soon. No pastor is eager to accept a call at a church with looming debt.

We set a date in October as "Harvest Day" at First Baptist. Our goal was to have 1,000 in Sunday school and to raise a special offering of $300,000 to pay off our debts. I told the church that if they would *get* us out of debt, I would *keep* us out. The plan was simple. We would emphasize "no empty chairs" in Sunday school that day. Then I asked every couple in church to give $100 a year for each year they had been married. My wife and I had been married 55 years, I explained, so our gift would need to be $5,500. I told the church I had already written my check and encouraged them to plan to do the same thing on Harvest Day. I reminded them that $100 a year was only a $1.97 a week or 27 cents a day. I quipped, "Men, where else can you get your meals cooked, clothes washed, house cleaned, and children cared for 27 cents a day?" Then I added, "You know your wives are worth every penny of it, so pay up!"

I encouraged every young person to give $25, the price of a hamburger, fries, and drink, each week for a month. I also asked every child to give $5 that they earned by doing extra work around the house. Of course, I knew not every family could afford that amount. There are always people living on Social Security and single parents who are getting by on a shoestring. The point was for all the people to do whatever they could do. I didn't want anybody to feel any pressure or guilt. The Scriptures say, "For if the willingness is there, the gift is acceptable according to what one has, not according to what he does not have," 2 Corinthians 8:12.

After a month of promotion, Harvest Day was upon us. The Saturday night prior it rained like I had not seen it rain before or since. The downpour continued when I went to bed, and I was confident that I would not sleep a wink knowing all of our efforts were going to be in vain. But to my amazement I went to sleep and did not wake up a single time all night long. That's the only time that has happened, and it was as if the Lord said to me, "Boy, go to sleep and rest. This is in my hands."

I woke up the next morning fearing disaster with the rain still pouring down. However, when we totaled the Sunday school attendance for both campuses, it was 956. Our total gifts were $620,000. Before the week was over, the gifts totaled $715,000! The church was out of debt, the budget was balanced, and we had a substantial cushion to carry us through the end of the year.

I had planned to tell the staff that it was a teachable moment for them, but I learned just as much about faith from the experience. It showed what a church is capable of accomplishing if they have a well-defined goal, a workable strategy, and enthusiastic promotion. At the close of the service the rain had stopped. As one of our members exited she said to me, "Thank you for helping us believe in ourselves again." By the end of the next year we had eradicated $2.2 million on a long-term debt, and the church had a balance of $200,000. Within a few months after that, the church had called a new pastor, signaling a new day in the life of an old church.

**

When I look back across the years, I can see the hand of God guiding and directing me when I thought I was in control and making my own decisions. I've already said it, but I need to say it just one more time: God works in mischievous ways. He had far more in store for me than I ever dreamed possible. Mine is and has been a blessed life.

I am not yet ready to write "The End" to the story quite yet, but I am ready and willing to sit down and watch that sunset any day that the Lord gives his permission. In the meantime I hope to be an encouragement to others and help some people along the way with what I've learned. As I think about the days I have left, I share the feelings expressed by the Apostle Paul as he bid farewell to the Ephesian elders. He was on his way to Jerusalem, and he did not know what was ahead. "I consider my life worth nothing to me, if only I may finish the race and complete the task the Lord Jesus has given me—the task of testifying to the gospel of God's grace," Acts 20:24.

Amen and amen!

Epilogue

I was standing at the back door of the First Baptist Church of Tyler where I was serving as interim pastor for a second time when a well-dressed young man came out to greet me. I had noticed him during the service. He sat on an aisle seat on the second row from the front, listening intensely to everything I said and watching my every move. His apparent interest in me made me interested in him.

As he came by, I introduced myself and found out he was a student at a small Missionary Baptist seminary in Jacksonville 30 miles away. He had read several of my books and said he was honored to meet me.

I responded, "No, no, I am the one who is honored. You young men are the hope of the future. I am an old man. I have had my day in the sun, and the sun is setting. You young men are the ones who have to take up the banner."

He then said with a smile, "We're ready, if you old men will just let go."

When I had finished greeting the people I turned to walk back to the front of the church. I thought to myself, "Lord, I'm ready and willing to let go when you give me permission." You see, when people say yes to God's call, they give up all right to self-determination. They are no longer their own but have been "bought with a price." The Lord now guides and directs their lives and their destinies.

How do you explain the call of God? You can't. Oswald Chambers said, "If you can explain God's call, you don't really have one!" It is a mystery from beginning to end. God calls us, "And no man taketh this honor unto himself," Hebrews 5:4. It is God who determines our destiny. His agenda is all that matters. And our duty is to trust and obey. My intention in writing this book was to simply bear witness to the fact that God does call, and when he calls, he guides and directs in astonishing ways.

At 83 years of age, I now find myself in the same position as Alexander Whyte, the majestic man who was the pastor of the greatest church in Edinburgh, Scotland, St. George's West. He was about 80 when he asked the Lord what he should do with the time he had left—should he retire or continue to preach? He then shared what happened:

"What seemed to me to be a divine respite with all-commanding power in my conscience said to me as clear as could be, 'No! Go on, and flinch not! Go back and boldly finish the work that has been given you to do. Speak out and fear not...no one else will so risk his life and his reputation...and you do not have much of either left to risk. Spend what is left of your life in your appointed task...'"

And that settles it for me. When writer Somerset Maugham was recuperating from the flu, an admirer called and asked, "Could I send you fruit, or would you prefer flowers?" He was 88 years old. He told her, "It is too late for fruit and too early for flowers."

It's been a long journey from the backwoods of East Texas to the back alleys of Port Arthur to the back of the class in school. But now I've tried to be upfront about my life story and how God led me on this path. The words of the Lord to Moses and the Children of Israel as they journeyed toward the Promised Land seem apropos: "The Lord thy God bare thee, as a man doth bear his son, in all the way that you went, until you came into this place," Deuteronomy 1:31. I've tried to carry the message, but all along he has carried me.

For all of this, I say thank you.

Powellisms

A collection of my favorite statements that, as far as I know, originated with me.

THE BIBLE

The old story must be told with a new freshness. The bread of life must not grow stale in us.

I always read from the King James Version. I'm from East Texas and the only thing we would use is the King James Version, red letter edition, Jimmy Swaggart autographed. Anything other than that is modernism.

We Baptists have no creed but the Bible, and I have signed every page of it. I don't intend to sign anything more, and I won't sign anything less.

Jude tells us that the faith was once delivered unto the saints. It was delivered unto us. We didn't discover the faith; we didn't develop the faith; we don't need to debate the faith. All we need to do is defend it and declare it.

I think people are fed up with not being fed in church.

CHURCH

God doesn't want any homeless children. Every Christian needs a church home.

If you want someone to stand up for you or kneel down with you, you will find it in this church.

COMMITMENT

What troubles me about the church today is not that the pews are half full or that the collection plates are half empty but that the people are half hearted.

CONFLICT

Don't ever knuckle under to a knucklehead.

There are two kinds of pain—you can have one, or you can be one. Some Christians are so mean if they were in the arena with the lions, I'd pull for the lions.

CONVERSION

It was on an ordinary Sunday, in an ordinary church, listening to an ordinary preacher preach an ordinary sermon when God did an extraordinary thing in my life. That's the way he ordinarily does it.

CULTURE

If I talked like they do on television today, my mother would have washed my mouth out with soap, and my dad would have knocked the suds out of me.

EARLY DEVOTIONALS/PIETY

If the Lord wanted us up before daylight, he'd have turned the lights on.

EXPERIENCE

I've been around the block a couple of times and up the alley once. I know what's going on.

FORGIVENESS

By God's grace we can forgive those who have let us down as Paul did, and those who knock us down as Stephen did, or those who nail us down as Jesus did.

We can forgive them and rise above them. We don't have to allow them to cause us to be bitter or a quitter. We don't have to allow the fact that they let us down get us down.

GOALS

The goal of most churches is to meet next Sunday, and they are always reaching their goal.

GROWING A CHURCH

Some things in the church are sacred. They assume the aura of sacredness like the Ark of the Covenant. You touch them and you die.

A dead church is a poor recommendation for a living Savior.

There are two kinds of pain in a church—growing pains and dying pains. Growing pains are better.

The church is not a business, but if it is not run like a business, it will soon be out of business.

Don't try to turn a rocking chair church into a rock-n-roll church.

We need to reach young people. It's hard to carry out the Great Commission sitting in a wheelchair or on a walker.

HANDLING HARD TIMES

If you, like Zacchaeus, find yourself up a tree and out on a limb, be assured that Jesus won't saw it off.

HARD WORK

Off your seat, on your feet, and into the street.

Some churches are filled with racehorses and others with plow horses. Both are perfectly good animals, they just move at a different gait. A racehorse is good for about five minutes. Hook a plow horse up early in the morning and when the sun is setting, he's still at the job.

When I surrendered to preach, no one told me you had to work weekends.

If we would wake up and get up, the church would fill up, and the world would sit up and take notice.

HUMILITY

I've eaten crow everyway it can be prepared—baked, stewed, barbequed, and fried extra crispy. I don't like it any way it's served. You may gag on it, but it won't kill you. In fact, sometimes it saves your life.

When people introduce me I usually say, "Keep it short. People aren't interested in all those details about my life and I already know them."

JESUS

When Jesus met the woman at the well, she had been married and divorced five times and now had a live-in boyfriend. But he didn't shun her. He saw her life, not so much in terms of badness, as sadness. She had flitted from man to man, marriage to marriage, relationship to relationship, looking for something she had never found. Her soul was as dry and as parched as ever. She needed living water.

When they told Jesus that the ruler's daughter was dead, he said, "She is not dead, she is asleep." They laughed him to scorn. They knew the difference between death and sleep, but they didn't know the difference between Jesus and other men.

JOY

Don't let the years, and the tears, and the jeers steal your joy and enthusiasm for life.

A dead church is a poor recommendation for a living Savior.

LEADERSHIP

If the preacher will let them, most churches will sit and do nothing and do it very well until Jesus comes. My people did nothing better than they did anything else.

If you have a better idea than mine, let's have it. I want to do things the best way possible. If you have no idea, let's do it my way.

Brains were God's idea. If he hadn't expected you to use your head, he would have given you two tail ends. He did give some people two tail ends.

Most churches are half-empty and fully satisfied.

MARRIAGE

When I go to a strange church to preach, Cathy often stays in the car to paint her nails and touch up her makeup while I go in and report for duty. If people ask about my wife I say, "She is in the car preparing the body for viewing."

MENTORING

Like Samuel, some children need an older and more experienced person to help them know when God is speaking to them.

MINISTERS

Preachers don't come out of the blue; they come out of the pew. They come out of people like you.

God Works in Mischievous Ways

MINISTRY

Our job as Christians is to take care of the saints...and the ain'ts.

MISSIONS

We need to make a great commotion over the Great Commission. To spend time on writing a new mission statement is an exercise in futility. Jesus gave us a mission statement in the Great Commission, and he didn't give us permission to change it.

No church needs to sit around and wonder why we are here or what we are to do. Jesus told us in the Great Commission. Our mission begins at the ends of our nose and our toes and goes and goes until we have told all men everywhere that Jesus saves.

MONEY

There are an awful lot of poor preachers...and some of them don't have any money.

While raising money for Truett I would sometimes say, "I need two things from you—prayer and money. If you

can do only one, give money. I'll get some old skinflint
to pray for us."

OLD AGE

I feel like an old tennis ball. I've been batted around
a lot, I've lost much of my bounce, but I'm still in the
game.

OUR NATION

When the former president of the United States is not
sure what the meaning of "is" is, we "is" in trouble.

Our national healing depends on our kneeling. We
must have revival for survival.

PERSEVERANCE

It is in the trenches that the ministry pinches.

PRIORITIES

You take care of God's kingdom, and he will take care of yours.

PREACHING

Z.N. Morrell was called "Wildcat Morrell." We need more wildcat preachers today. We've got too many tomcat preachers—women chasers; pussycat preachers—lazing around and wanting to be petted; hip-cat preachers—chasing every new fad; and polecat preachers—real stinkers. We need more wildcats.

Preaching is both a gift and a discipline. Good preaching takes a lot of hard work. In fact, if you don't work hard, no one will ever know that you have the gift.

I've often said in jest, "My sermons warmed over are better than most preachers' hot off the griddle."

I've preached everywhere once and one place twice.

REDEMPTION

What we need is not to turn over a new leaf in life. We need to have the old pages washed clean. God has a big eraser and it doesn't leave any smudges.

SATAN

I know the devil is real. I've done business with him before.

SERVING OTHERS

Most Christians want to sit, soak, and sour until the Second Coming. We need to be serving.

You can sit in a pew until you mildew.

The church suffers from a labor shortage today. Why is that? When you add up those who are washed out, burned out, thrown out, and found out, it is easy to understand.

SIN

He was so big a sinner it left a ring around the baptistery when I baptized him.

Sin—if you'll admit it and quit it, God will forget it.

VISITATION

I said in greeting visitors every Sunday in the congregation, "If you would like a visit from the pastor, indicate it on the card. I can't visit everyone, but I sure can visit you."

WORSHIP

We need to sing the old songs with a new spirit. But we must sing with our hearts and not just with our lips.

We need more woe-is-me and less whoopee in our worship.

We don't need "Whoopee" Goldberg churches, but neither do we need iceberg churches.

There are several kinds of churches—mausoleum churches, museum churches, and coliseum churches. Mausoleums are resting places for the dead. Museums are preservers of the past. Coliseums are entertainment centers for spectators. We need to be Spirit-filled churches.

The mark of a Spirit-filled church is not that the congregation does the "holy wave" on Sunday. It is not that the church has a pastor who can knock your socks off with his preaching. It is not that the church has a choir that rivals a Broadway production. It is something much deeper than that.